CONTENTS

Ships in Focus Publications

Correspondence and editorial:
Roy Fenton
18 Durrington Avenue
London SW20 8NT
020 8879 3527
record@rfenton.co.uk

Orders and photographic:
John & Marion Clarkson
18 Franklands, Longton
Preston PR4 5PD
01772 612855
shipsinfocus@btinternet.com

Printed by Amadeus Press Ltd.,
Cleckheaton, Yorkshire.
Designed by Hugh Smallwood, John Clarkson
and Roy Fenton.

SHIPS IN FOCUS RECORD
ISBN 978-0-9928263-2-1

SUBSCRIPTION RATES FOR RECORD

Readers can start their subscription with any
issue, and are welcome to backdate it to receive
previous issues.

	3 issues	4 issues
UK	£27	£35
Europe (airmail)	£29	£38
Rest of the world (surface mail)	£29	£38
Rest of the world (airmail)	£35	£46

SHIPS IN FOCUS

November

CW01461208

There's nothing a researcher likes b[etter than nailing]
an incorrect piece of published hist[ory. The United]
States schooner *A.B. Sherman* is ce[rtainly featured]
in the feature on Fowey's powered coasters in this issue. Writing of this
vessel, Ward Jackson, the author of the otherwise excellent 'Ships and
Shipbuilders of a West Country Port', claims that she was captured by the
Royal Navy during the First World War whilst supplying a U-boat near the
Scillies. This seemed most unlikely. Granted, the incident happened just
before the United States entered the war, but just how could a pure sailing
vessel, which would not even have a radio, rendezvous so precisely with
a submarine, and why in British waters? It was reminiscent of the claims,
current during and after the Second World War, of U-boats being resupplied
in the waters of neutral Eire, stories which have been convincingly refuted.
It is not surprising that these myths arose, given the fear, amounting almost
to terror, which the submarine gave rise to in these conflicts, and which
weapon the Royal Navy was very largely unprepared to counter for much of
the First World War.

Nailing the myth about *A.B. Sherman* fell to Bill Schell, co-
author of the Starke-Schell registers. Using published sources, he readily
established that the schooner had been *attacked* by the submarine *UC 62*,
which first shelled her and then placed scuttling charges on board, only to
be interrupted by the arrival of a steamer, probably naval. This explained
why *A.B. Sherman* was so badly damaged that post-war repairs took several
years and were ruinously expensive. The moral is: use one's critical
faculties when reading maritime (and other) history. And that also goes for
material in 'Record'!

More First World War action, which took place exactly one
hundred years ago this November, is the subject of Andrew Bell's article
on the merchant ships which, one way or another, became embroiled in the
battles of Coronel and the Falklands. It is salutary to remember, as Andrew
points out, that Coronel was the first time for over one hundred years that
the Royal Navy had been convincingly beaten in battle. Although the defeat
was swiftly and brilliantly avenged, this plus the ambiguous outcome of big
battles like Jutland and not least the abject failure for three years to counter
the depredations of U-boats begs the question, did the world's largest and
most powerful navy really perform that well during the First World War?
This journal is concerned principally with merchant ship matters, but the
evidence is there in so many of our accounts of First World War merchant ship
losses that, until politicians belatedly compelled the Admiralty to institute a
convoy system, Britain's ability to feed itself and supply its armed forces was
being put at serious risk, and the lives of thousands of civilian seamen were
being sacrificed. No doubt this particular piece of revisionism will evoke
comments from our readership!

John Clarkson   Roy Fenton

One of the protagonists in the Battle of the Falklands, which avenged the
defeat at Coronel, was P&O's *Macedonia*, which was serving as an armed
merchant cruiser. See pages 130 to 135. *[Ian J. Farquhar collection]*

Unaware that war had broken out, *Induna* (699/1891) of Burns, Philp and Co. Ltd. stumbled into Admiral Graf von Spee's squadron in the Marshall Islands in August 1914. The Aberdeen-built steamer survived a brief internment to return to Australia, where she had a variety of further owners, including the Railway Commissioners for New South Wales who converted her to a train ferry. Laid up in 1932 at Grafton, New South Wales, dismantling began in 1934, but it was not until 1957 that demolition was completed. *[Ian J. Farquahar collection]*

Cunard's Clydebank-built turbine steamer *Carmania* (19,524/1905) is seen at the Prince's Landing Stage, Liverpool. Her requisition as an armed merchant cruiser ended in July 1916, when she returned to Cunard, although she was then heavily involved in trooping. She was broken up by Hughes, Bolckow at Blyth where she arrived on 22nd April 1932. *[B. and A. Feilden/J. and M. Clarkson]*

MERCHANT SHIPS AT CORONEL AND AFTER
Andrew Bell

One morning in early August 1914 Captain Webster, in command of Burns, Philp's *Induna*, brought the ship to anchor in the lagoon at Jaluit in the Marshall Islands. The master and Mr. Walford his chief engineer were surprised to find Admiral von Spee's fleet of warships and numerous German merchant ships in port: they concluded that there was some sort of celebration going on; was this Kiel Regatta Week being held at a German colonial tropical island? Burns, Philp's captains were often more notable than the ships that they commanded. The Sydney-based Pacific trading company was often expanding, adding to or replacing their ships from the sale and purchase market. The *Induna* had been purchased in 1904 to be used on Burns Philp's service between Sydney and the Gilbert and Ellice Islands and the Marshall Islands. She was not equipped with radio. An often-forgotten section of modern history is that, before the First World War, Germany had colonised the Marshalls, the Carolines and part of New Guinea. To the surprise of all on board the *Induna* what the Germans were celebrating was the outbreak of war. Having been required to sell the *Induna*'s bunker coal to the German Navy the ship was impounded until the Japanese, on the Allies' side, liberated Jaluit in late September.

Von Spee's fleet had been based at the Chinese treaty port of Tsingtao (now Qingdao) but by design most of the fleet were not there on 4th August 1914: they had sailed out into the vast Pacific. At the British treaty port of Wei-Hai-Wei, Admiral Jerram, in command of the five ships of East Indies Station fleet, was woefully short of useful intelligence about the whereabouts of the five-ship German fleet. Both fleets had numerous colliers for, at least in the Pacific, this was still the age of coal-fired, steam-engined ships, and both fleets had only rudimentary radio communications equipment. Throughout the next three months a game of hide and seek was played out amongst the atolls and islands of the Pacific. The first object of the opponents was to cut communications. The Germans raided Fanning Island on 7th September destroying everything servicing the cable linking Canada and New Zealand. The German colonies had largely centred all their communications, both cable and radio, at Yap in the Pelew group. On 12th August, after due warning to minimise civilian casualties, HMS *Hampshire* destroyed all the communication facilities at Yap.

Escapes and evasions

Unable to break the German Navy's code, the gathering fleets of Australia, New Zealand, France and Japan, plus the Royal Navy displayed an intensity of effort which was not matched with finding and confronting von Spee's squadron and its two principal ships, *Gneisenau* and *Scharnhorst*. Von Spee headed eastwards having detached *Emden* to prey on the shipping routes of the Indian Ocean with such effect that Allied merchant shipping movements were all but paralysed. Even a German gunboat played a part in one of the strangest maritime adventures of the war. On 4th September *Geier* found a British tramp ship owned by the Lewis Trading Co. Ltd. of Cardiff, the *Southport* (3,585/1900) loading copra as it became available at Kusaig in the Eastern Carolines. She

was unaware that war had broken out. Having disabled his prize the captain of the gunboat set off on a fortnight's cruise through the rest of the archipelago. The *Southport*'s Captain Clopet and Chief Engineer Mr H. Cox were determined to escape and there followed one of the great stories of the merchant navy's war. The official report relates:

'Desperate as was the chance and short the time, the crew agreed and, under the clever chief engineer, they set to work to repair the engines, in spite of the almost hopeless condition to which they had been reduced. The eccentric gear of the main and high-pressure engines and the intermediate stop valve had been removed as well as a good many tools, but after eleven days work, by fitting the astern eccentric of the low-pressure engine to the high-pressure cylinder, and cutting out the middle cylinder, they got a semblance of a compound engine. True, it would not go astern, and if it was stopped might get on a dead centre and refuse to start again. Nor was this the only trouble. They had over 2,000 miles to go to reach a British port, and no provisions except what the island – which, like the rest, was not self-supporting – could provide. However, from the native king, whom the Germans had told to help him with food, Captain Clopet obtained 350 coconuts and 400 lbs of a root the natives ate only in time of famine. With this equipment, after infinite difficulty in getting their unhandy craft to sea, they started on 18th September with only a day in hand. Still, they escaped arriving at Brisbane on 30th September. The exploit was recognised by an Admiralty letter expressing high appreciation of the captain's and the engineer's seamanlike and skilful conduct, and to each the Board of Trade presented a piece of silverware.'

In September there had been one of the few full-blooded actions between two armed merchant ships adapted as auxiliary cruisers of the war. Cunard's *Carmania* happened upon Hamburg Sud's *Cap Trafalgar* (18,805/1914) coaling at Trinidada Island off the Brazilian coast. During the exchange of fire modern explosives wreaked havoc in both ships' combustible accommodation whilst untrained crews proved just how vulnerable were merchant ships converted for war. The German ship sank and the Cunarder was extensively damaged, on fire, and was saved by the ship handling talents of Captain Noel Grant RN. The liner's pre-war master, Captain J.C. Barr, was on board as navigator and adviser, and received the CB for his role in the action.

Before the Panama Canal opened fully on 16th August 1914 the Pacific Steam Navigation Company's route from Liverpool to the west coast of South America was via the Magellan Straits. On 16th September 1914 the company's *Ortega* left Valparaiso homeward bound with, amongst her passengers, 300 French nationals who were military reservists. Three days later as she proceeded down the coastline of the Chilean fjords and their spectacular backdrop of the high Andes, the *Ortega* was challenged by a three-funnelled cruiser identified as hostile: it was *Dresden*. Captain Douglas Kinnier knew that at 15 knots he could not outrun the German cruiser and took the decision which was one that came from another age. The *Ortega* turned eastwards for the Cambridge Islands (now known as Diego

Another classic Mersey photograph depicts Pacific Steam Navigation's Belfast-built *Ortega* (7,970/1906). She escaped requisition in August 1914, and continued on her owner's routes to the west coast of South America. *Ortega* arrived at Briton Ferry to be broken up by T.W. Ward Ltd. on 27th June 1927. *[B. and A. Feilden/J. and M. Clarkson]*

de Alamagro) behind which lay the northern entrance of the Nelson Strait: the German cruiser dared not follow for the passage was uncharted. In his official report Captain Kinnier wrote: 'The narrow, tortuous passage constitutes a veritable nightmare for navigation bristling as it does with reefs and pinnacle rocks, swept by fierce currents and tide rips, with cliffs on either side sheer and without any anchorages'. One hundred miles south the *Ortega* emerged into the Smyth Channel. So sure were the Chileans that the *Ortega* would have foundered that they sent a naval ship to search for survivors. Promoted to be an RNR lieutenant commander, Captain Kinnier was awarded the DSC in recognition of this feat of valuable evasion.

Towards Coronel

Into October 1914 the area of action was switching south eastwards in the Pacific and the strategically important Straits of Magellan and Cape Horn where winter conditions were lingering. At last anticipating von Spee's plans, the British Admiralty ordered Admiral Sir Christopher Cradock (1862-1914) in command of the South Atlantic Station's ships to move towards Chilean waters. Cradock assembled his scratch fleet to intercept but without knowledge of von Spee's whereabouts or that of two German cruisers that had started their war in the Caribbean. *Dresden* and *Karlsruhe* were heading south towards Cape Horn but hid their course so well and such was the fear of the German navy's reputation that the ports of the River Plate were crowded with merchant ships afraid to sail.

The British met von Spee's ships off Coronel on 1st November 1914; there followed an unequal battle.

It was summarised as one 'in which a weak composite British squadron – inferior in armament, age of the ships and speed – was matched against a crack experienced fast German force'. The British lost *Good Hope* (including the Admiral) and *Monmouth* but *Glasgow* plus the armed merchant cruiser *Otranto* escaped under cover of darkness being only slightly damaged. 'It was the first severe British naval reverse for over a century and, worst of all, the command of the seas from Panama to Cape Horn passed into enemy hands', recorded Winston Churchill. This was soon apparent as Allied ships were intercepted and sunk, one of the first being the Admiralty's chartered collier *North Wales* (3,691/1905). The German cruisers *Leipzig* and the collier/storeship *Baden* (7,676/1913) captured and made prizes of two ships both laden with Welsh coal; they were the French four-masted barque *Valentine* (2,686/1901) with 3,000 tons and the Norwegian *Helicon* (1,640/1887) with 1,600 tons. At this stage of the German squadron's progress von Spee's main refuelling base was San Quentin Sound, a deserted bay in the Chilean Gulf of Penne, 300 miles north of the Magellan Straits. Arriving there on 21st November, waiting for the squadron was Norddeutscher Lloyd's *Seydlitz* (8,002/1902), Kosmos Line's *Memphis* (7,074/1913) and the *Luxor* (7,109g/1913) which, flouting Chilean neutrality, had loaded 3,000 tons of coal – part of a stem of 9,500 tons – before the authorities at Coronel put a stop to it and she sailed for the rendezvous in the south. The *Luxor*'s departure was reported by the local British agent to the Admiralty which, at last, gave confirmation that von Spee was preparing to break out of the Pacific and into the South Atlantic. During the four months of crossing

Orient Line's *Otranto* (12,124/1909) was built by Workman, Clark and Co. Ltd., Belfast. Serving as an armed merchant cruiser since early August 1914, she was fortunate to escape from the Battle of Coronel with only minor damage. However, she was to become one of the last, and most tragic, merchant ship casualties of the First World War. On 6th October 1918 she was bringing United States troops to Liverpool when she collided with P&O's *Kashmir* (8,841/1915). *Otranto* drifted ashore on Islay, the death toll being 431. *[Ian J. Farquhar collection]*

the Pacific the German East Asiatic Squadron had sunk the merchant ships *Hyades* (3,552/1899) and the *Holmwood* (4,223/1912) in August; the *Elsinore* (6,500/1913) and *Bankfields* (3,763g/1905) in September; the *North Wales* and the French barque in November.

At the Admiralty the rout at Coronel had an instant effect on Winston Churchill as First Lord and Sir John (later Lord) 'Jackie' Fisher, the First Sea Lord. On 5th November the battle cruisers *Invincible* and *Inflexible* were withdrawn from the Grand Fleet and, after a furious and fast refit and replenishment at Devonport, sailed on 11th November under the command of Vice Admiral Sir Doveton Sturdee (1859-1925). The dash to the South Atlantic was on in circumstances as secret as it was possible to be. After a brief call at St Vincent in the Cape Verde Islands the pair arrived at Abrolhos Rocks, a position 120 miles north of Rio de Janeiro, meeting Rear Admiral Stoddart with *Carnarvon, Cornwall, Bristol, Kent* and the armed merchant cruiser *Orama* (12,927/1911) and, finally refitted at Rio, the Coronel survivor *Glasgow*.

A product of J. Blumer and Co., Sunderland, *Hyades* (3,552/1899) was owned by the British and South American Steam Navigation Co. Ltd., better known as the Houston Line. Her sinking on 15th August 1914 is credited to SMS *Dresden*, in a position 180 miles north east by a quarter north of Pernambuco whilst on a voyage from Rosario to Rotterdam with a cargo of maize. *[Roy Fenton collection]*

Prelude to the Falklands

On 15th November whilst still at anchor in his Chilean fjord hideout von Spee received a telegram from the German Vice-Consul at Punta Arenas which overlooks the Magellan Strait: it was one that changed the course of history. It advised that a passing British steamer had reported that there were no warships at Stanley, capital of the Falkland Islands. What von Spee did not know was that on 12th November the first of the British warships, the out-of-date battleship *Canopus,* had arrived there. On this news von Spee decided to occupy the Falklands: there is some evidence that he would then propose to Berlin that the islands should be handed over to Argentina. Messages were sent to mobilise German volunteer forces in two Latin American countries. German agents in Montevideo were instructed to load the *Eleonore Woermann* (4,624/1902) and the *Mera* (4,797/1901) with construction equipment and provisions: a German baron resident in Chile was said to have been appointed as acting governor. The occupation of the Falklands was not a decision taken with the unanimous support of the captains of von Spee's squadron. Von Spee disregarded an intelligence report that two British cruisers had been seen passing Pernambuco, Brazil southwards on 30th November – he decided this was a British deception: it was another fatal mistake. As his fleet approached Orange Bay in the Beagle Channel just north of Cape Horn on 2nd December they met the Canadian-owned sailing vessel *Drummuir* (l,719/1882) carrying 2,800 tons of coal that had been loaded at Cardiff for San Francisco. With no sense of urgency, four days were taken to distribute the prize's coal to top up the squadrons' bunkers. The *Drummuir* was towed out into deep water and scuttled. On the day von Spee sailed for the Falklands, Admiral Sturdee's squadron arrived at Stanley.

Right up until 09:20 on the morning of 8th December von Spee thought that the Falkland Islands were lightly defended and its capital, doubling as a British naval base, was his for the taking. It was at that time that he sighted activity and smoke as he made a landfall off Stanley: his surmise that stocks of coal were being destroyed was very wrong. The recently arrived British warships were coaling in Stanley's outer harbour together with *Carnarvon* and *Cornwall*: *Glasgow* and *Bristol* were in the inner harbour and purposely grounded (to enhance the firm firing of her guns) was *Canopus*. P&O's armed merchant cruiser *Macedonia* was at sea on patrol and about to be relieved by *Kent*. The story goes that two housemaids hanging out the morning's washing at Fitzroy were the first to see the vanguard ships, *Gneisenau* and *Nurnburg*. Their employer, one Mrs Felton, telephoned the news to town and her reward was, later, to be a tea service presented to her by the Admiralty. Unseen to von Spee *Canopus* fired the first shot over the isthmus of land between Stanley and Cape Pembroke peninsula. It was a ranging shot and fell short of the pair of German ships: the Battle of the Falkland Islands had opened. What caused the two ships to turn hard aport away from Stanley Harbour approaches and head southwards was the unexpected sighting of tripod masts in the outer harbour. Within two hours six British

P&O's *Macedonia* (10,512/1904) had been built by Harland and Wolff Ltd. and, as was their current practice, the line registered her at the port of her building, Belfast. She was requisitioned by the Admiralty immediately on the outbreak of war, and fitted with eight 4.7-inch guns, later replaced with 6-inch weapons. Her early patrols in the South Atlantic, with her participation in two sinkings, were the major excitements of her naval career, and no further actions are reported. She was purchased by the Admiralty in 1917, continuing as an armed merchant cruiser until the Armistice, when she was converted to a troop ship. Reconditioned by the Royal Navy at Portsmouth she returned to P&O in September 1921 until sold for demolition in Yokohama during 1931. Breakers were Amakasu Gomei Kaisha who took delivery of her at Osaka on 4th November1931 after she had made a P&O voyage to the Far East from Tilbury. *[Roy Fenton collection]*

warships were at sea following a 'general chase' order. Pursuing the Germans at his ships' maximum speed 'open fire' was signalled at 12:51 and the battle lasted four hours by which time four out of the five German ships had been successively destroyed, an action on the Royal Navy's part achieved by superior equipment, ship handling (often hampered by large amount of coal smoke) and battle tactics. Not only had the Kaiser lost four ships but also the lives of von Spee, two of his sons, and 2,196 seamen – just 225 survivors were rescued by the victors. Only *Dresden* escaped, heading back to the Pacific; she was cornered by *Glasgow* at Mas-a-Tierra on 14th March 1915 and destroyed either by accident or by her crew's intent.

In a secondary action *Bristol* and the *Macedonia* pursued the German fleet train of merchant ships that had been ordered towards the Falklands with the intention of entering Port Pleasant to await another von Spee victory. They were the *Baden* and the *Santa Isabel* (5,199/1914): a third ship the *Seydlitz* (7,942/1903) had been ordered to standby and act as a hospital ship. The first pair were taken at 15:00 and found to be still loaded with cargoes of coal and stores: both ships were needlessly sunk because Captain Fanshaw did not question Admiral Sturdee's standing order 'sink the transports' despite the value and usefulness of their cargoes. The *Seydlitz* escaped. The *Macedonia* landed the captured German crews back in Stanley where, in the harbour, witness to the events of the day were the merchant ships *Benbrook* (3,840/1910), *Trelawney* (3,877/1907), *Benguela* (5,520/1910), and the *Errington Court* (4,461/1909).

Perhaps the strangest event of that summer day in the South Atlantic was that of a full-rigged ship that sailed through the opposing squadrons during the afternoon. This was the *Fairport* (1,996/1896) homeward bound from Tocopilla in Northern Chile. She had recently been transferred by Richard Salvesen of Leith to their Norwegian subsidiary at Tvedestrand. Remaining on board to complete their indentures were two British apprentices, one of these A.D. Rogers (later to become Air Commodore) was a midshipman RNR who had the frustration of not being part of a naval battle but witnessing it from the main cross-trees of a neutral sailing ship.

It can be reflected that the battle of the Falkland Islands, one hundred years ago, was even further removed from the navies of 2014 - with their electronic warfare and nuclear propulsion - than were those of von Spee's and Sturdee's from the sailing ships that fought at Trafalgar one hundred and nine years before.

Two merchant ship witnesses to the Battle of the Falklands were Elder, Dempster's *Benguela* (5,520/1910) (upper) and *Errington Court* (4,461/1909) (lower). The *Benguela* had been built by Swan, Hunter and Wigham Richardson Ltd. on the Tyne, and survived the war but not the subsequent depression. On 20th June 1933 she arrived on the river of her birth to load coal for Italy, where she was sold for breaking up, possibly at Bari.

The tramp steamer *Errington Court* was a more likely visitor to Port Stanley than the Elder, Dempster cargo liner. Also completed on the Tyne, she came from the yard of the Northumberland Shipbuilding Co. Ltd. and was delivered to Court Line Ltd., managed by Haldinstein and Co. (who were in 1916 to change their name to the less Germanic-sounding Haldin and Co.). Sale in 1919 saw her go to other British owners as *Bournemouth*, and from there she went to Greece as *Despina*, and in 1938 to Wheelock, Marden and Co. who registered her in Shanghai as *Deslock*. She was unfortunate enough to be in Yokohama in December 1941, and was seized by the Japanese who renamed her *Uzan Maru*. Alas, her career had less than six months to run. The Submarine USS *Trout* torpedoed her south of Honshu on 2nd May 1942. *[Roy Fenton collection; Ships in Focus]*

SOUTHERN RAILWAY CARGO SHIPS 1923-1947
Part 1
John de S. Winser

The 1923 consolidation of Britain's railways into four major groupings resulted in the new Southern Railway Company inheriting a fleet which included 14 British-registered cross-Channel cargo steamers, operating from Dover, Folkestone and Southampton. In 1922 these vessels had carried a mere 8,300 tons of cargo across the Strait of Dover for the South Eastern and Chatham Railway and slightly less than 13,000 tons for the London and South Western Railway between Southampton and ports on the Continent and in the Channel Islands. The state of this inheritance can be assessed from the fact that, with 25 years being regarded as a ship's lifespan, the cargo fleet's average age was one year in excess of that, with one ship, *Cherbourg*, being 50 years old and another, *C.W. Eborall*, over 40. In these circumstances, it was unsurprising that at the earliest opportunity the company should authorise the start of a massive shipbuilding programme. It was a programme which was to prove unprecedented in railway shipping history, introducing into service no fewer than nine similar vessels over a period of five years. Concentrating almost exclusively on their days in Southern Railway ownership, these articles highlight incidents and events relating to the 14 inherited steamers, then goes on to outline the story of the nine new ships and concludes by describing two later vessels, the first of which was a development of the original nine. The second of the two was a war loss replacement delivered on the eve of the company going out of existence at the end of December 1947 as a result of railway nationalisation.

Inheritance replaced

The 1882-built *C.W. Eborall* was one of six railway cargo ships in service across the Strait of Dover in early summer 1923. She was employed on a daily round trip between Dover and Calais in conjunction with *Deal* and *Canterbury*, which were 27 and 22 years old respectively. *Canterbury* was on occasion allocated outward shipments of wool but was primarily employed on the cross-Channel conveyance of the Indian mails, carried by rail between Calais and Marseilles and thence by ship to Bombay. The steamers *Folkestone*, which first sailed into Dover harbour in 1903, and *Walmer*, which had been in railway service since 1894, were each performing single daily crossings between Folkestone and Boulogne in May 1923, augmented by the 1899-built *Maidstone* which was making frequent outward sailings in ballast in order to return the same day with full cargoes of fruit and vegetables. In August that year the crew of *Folkestone* distinguished themselves by successfully rescuing five French seamen whose vessel had foundered in heavy seas. It was at the end of October 1923 that the Southern Railway authorised the seeking of tenders for the replacement of all six vessels of its Strait of Dover cargo fleet, at the rate of two ships per annum, starting with the oldest, *C W Eborall* and *Walmer*. The new construction work was contracted to D. and W. Henderson at Glasgow who had the first vessel in frame by the end of February 1924. The very next month *C.W. Eborall* left Dover for the breaker's yard, following her retirement early the previous December

The 1896-built cargo steamer *Deal* is alongside her Folkestone berth as one of the five railway passenger ships of *The Queen* class pulls away for Boulogne. *[A.M.S. Russell collection]*

In the centre of this view of Folkestone is *Walmer*, which served the railways from 1894 until 1935. The paddle steamer alongside her is the excursion vessel *Myleta*. [A.M.S. Russell collection]

because of leaks, and a temporarily chartered vessel was used until the Southampton ship *Vena* could provisionally fill the gap at the end of March 1924.

In July the fleet strength was restored by the introduction of the new *Tonbridge*, admirably suited to the Folkestone-Boulogne route, because of her capacity for carrying horses and the ability to cope with the rapid handling of all classes of cargo. With a crew of 20 and a cargo capacity in excess of 30,000 cubic feet, the twin-screw, coal-burner was designed to be suitable for service on all the company's routes, subject to the modification of horse fittings and internal arrangements. She was followed in August by *Minster*, whose service between Folkestone and Boulogne got off to a shaky start, owing to the almost immediate requirement for repairs after a defect prevented her engines from going astern.

February 1925 saw the sale for demolition of *Maidstone*, which had seven months previously become the first of the Dover fleet to wear the Southern Railway's newly-adopted funnel colouring of buff with black top. In a reversal of the original plan, *Walmer* was given what proved to be a decade's reprieve, despite her age and her need for substantial stem repairs, after being involved in a serious collision with Admiralty Pier, when arriving at Dover from Boulogne. Early in June 1925 came Henderson's next product, *Hythe*, followed in August by *Whitstable*, a name adopted one month before her launching in place of the original choice of *Bexhill*. The addition of these two new ships cleared the way for the subsequent disposal of *Deal* and *Canterbury* and the fifth new vessel,

reviving the name *Maidstone*, joined the fleet at the end of April 1926, seven months prior to the sale of *Folkestone* for conversion to a private yacht. This, rather surprisingly, had also been the immediate post-railway career of *Canterbury*, which did not end her days until the mid-1950s, having latterly been employed on commercial service in South American waters. The accompanying table shows that *Walmer* was in a sufficiently good state to complete a greater number of Channel crossings than any other member of the cargo fleet in 1927, a year during which Southern Railway cargo steamers exported from Dover and Folkestone in excess of 46,000 tons of cargo. The imported tonnage of machinery and other items that year totalled 28,600 at Dover, while the equivalent figure for Folkestone

Seen here in Dover's Wellington Dock, *Maidstone* was one of the class of nine similar vessels to join the Southern Railway cargo fleet between 1924 and 1928. [National Maritime Museum N35564]

In 1929, *Whitstable* introduced a new service carrying cars across the Channel. The cars' drivers and their passengers crossed aboard the passenger steamers. *[National Maritime Museum N38148]*

was 62,240, made up not only of fruit and vegetables but also of cottons, silks, woollens and yarns, wines and spirits. These were massive increases compared with the meagre totals of 1922 mentioned earlier. Another important cargo, confined almost exclusively to the Folkestone-Boulogne route, was the movement of horses, with 2,268 being exported in 1927 and 617 imported, *Whitstable* being able to accommodate a total of 62. A sixth new ship, perpetuating the name *Deal*, was delivered in April 1928 after being delayed for repairs, having, on a foggy March night, become stranded on rocks during the early stages of her post-trials delivery voyage.

Accidents are at times inevitable when attempting to operate cross-Channel services in all weathers and many of the cargo ships sustained damage of some sort during their service careers. None were probably quite as avoidable as when the Southampton vessel *Bertha*, coming alongside at her home port in January 1923, heavily rammed the quayside as a result of her chief engineer setting the engines to go ahead instead of astern.

New steamers for Southampton

In January 1925, the company took the decision to order two new cargo steamers for the Southampton fleet. They were destined to be replacements for three uneconomical units, *Rina* and *Vena*, which had first entered commercial service in 1902 but had only been in railway ownership since 1922, and *Laura*, which had started her days in 1885 as a passenger vessel but had been relegated to cargo ship status in the winter of 1921-1922. For retention were five single-screw vessels: the 1895 *Ulrica*, which was purchased by the railways in 1919 and was fitted to carry cattle; the 1873 *Cherbourg*; the 1905 sisters *Ada* and *Bertha*, as well as the 1910 *Brittany* which had initially sailed between Newhaven and Caen for the London, Brighton and South Coast Railway. The two replacement vessels, both delivered ahead of their expected dates, were *Haslemere* in July 1925, two days after achieving 16 knots on her trials, and *Fratton* in September, after a change from the original name choice of *Lyndhurst*.

They were followed in October 1925 by the ordering of a third new ship for the Southampton routes: carrying the name *Ringwood*, the new steamer arrived in mid-June 1926. The following year *Ringwood* accounted for just over 24,000 of the 179,813 nautical miles sailed by the nine Southampton cargo ships, which between them carried almost 35,000 tons of outward shipments, around three quarters destined for the Channel Islands. The most productive loading port for Southern Railway cargo inbound to Southampton that year was St Malo which contributed more than 40% of the 180,733-ton total, with 23% coming from the Channel Islands and the remainder being loaded at Cherbourg, Honfleur and Le Havre. More than

Ringwood was ordered by the Southern Railway for Southampton services. *[J. and M. Clarkson]*

Number of single Channel crossings performed by each vessel, January 1927 to December 1932							
Name of vessel	1927	1928	1929	1930	1931	1932	Total
Dover and Folkestone services (route length – up to 26 nautical miles)							
Autocarrier (new 3.1931)	-	-	-	436	464	900	1,800
Deal (new 4.1928)	-	151	312	432	396	331	1,622
Hythe	247	288	296	372	365	301	1,869
Maidstone	270	291	246	311	344	347	1,809
Minster	269	226	370	348	289	267	1,769
Tonbridge	274	332	352	377	355	278	1,968
Walmer	318	94	185	265	243	190	1,295
Whitstable	305	305	517	528	412	253	2,320
Total	1,683	1,687	2,278	2,633	2,840	2,431	
Southampton services (route length – up to 151 nautical miles)							
Ada	174	187	126	180	145	91	903
Bertha	173	170	136	174	144	72	869
Brittany	186	142	179	177	155	105	944
Cherbourg	163	175	163	*	-	-	501
Fratton	169	188	186	174	166	111	994
Haslemere	163	196	178	180	140	141	998
Laura	147	*	-	-	-	-	147
Ringwood	190	152	198	179	169	129	1,017
Ulrica	79	*	-	-	-	-	79
Total	1,444	1,210	1,166	1,064	919	649	
*No longer in Southern Railway service							

1,600 head of cattle left the Channel Islands for the mainland, *Ringwood* being specially adapted to accommodate 136 in her forward hold and a further 46 aft. In this capacity she was replacing *Ulrica*, which was withdrawn in 1927 and subsequently broken up to eliminate the expense of essential repairs.

To be concluded

Fleet list part 1: vessels taken over by the Southern Railway in 1923

The Act of Parliament setting up the Southern Railway was dated 22nd December 1922, but formal re-registration of the ships in the new company's name occurred only on 25th April 1923 for the former South Eastern and Chatham Railway ships and on 21st June 1923 for those of the former London and South Western and the London, Brighton and South Coast Railways. However, for the purposes of this list all ships are reckoned to have joined the Southern Railway fleet on the day the company formally took over services, 1st January 1923. The ships are listed in order of their building dates.

1. CHERBOURG 1923-1930 Iron
O.N. 68826 388g 191n.
165.6 x 23.1 x 11.9 feet.
Cargo capacity 21,080 cubic feet.
C. 2-cyl. by Smith Brothers and Co., Glasgow; 65 NHP, 12 knots.
1897: T.3-cyl. by J.P. Rennoldson and Son, South Shields; 75 NHP, 650 IHP, 12 knots.

Built for the London and South Western Railway in 1873, *Cherbourg* was the oldest cargo steamer taken into the Southern Railway fleet in 1923. *[Dave Hocquard collection]*

10.1873: Launched by J. and R. Swan, Dumbarton (Yard No. 82).
1883: Delivered to the London and South Western Railway Company, Southampton as CHERBOURG at a cost of £12,855.
1897: Re-engined.
1.1.1923: Transferred to the Southern Railway Company, London for Strait of Dover services.
1930: Sold to G. and W. Brunton, Grangemouth for £900 for breaking up during the first quarter.
20.10.1931: Register closed.

2. C.W. EBORALL 1923-1924 Iron
O.N. 87039 452g 217n.
190.2 x 25.1 x 12.0 feet.
C. 2-cyl. by Earle's Shipbuilding and Engineering Co. Ltd., Hull; 110 NHP, 10 knots.
14.12.1882: Launched by Earle's Shipbuilding and Engineering Co. Ltd., Hull (Yard No. 257).
16.1.1883: Registered in the ownership of the South Eastern Railway Company, London as C.W. EBORALL.
10.7.1900: Transferred to the South

Eastern and Chatham Railway Companies' Managing Committee, London
1.1.1923: Transferred to the Southern Railway for Strait of Dover services.
1924: Sold to J.W. Bagley for £1,100 for breaking up.
1.3.1924: Register closed.

3. LAURA 1923-1927
O.N. 90415 592g 223n.
207.0 x 26.8 x 13.3 feet.
C. 2-cyl. by J. and J. Thomson, Glasgow; 205 NHP, 14 knots.
20.3.1885: Launched by Aitken and Mansel, Glasgow (Yard No. 132).
5.1885: Completed for the London and South Western Railway Company, London as the passenger vessel LAURA at a cost of £23,500.
1921-22: Converted to cargo ship.
1.1.1923: Transferred to the Southern Railway Company, London for Southampton services.
6-7.11.1925: Lost rudder head 30 miles off Cap de la Hague whilst on passage from St Malo to Southampton and taken in tow to Southampton.
1.12.1925: Struck French ketch TALBURG at Guernsey.
1927: Sold to Captain Yeazel of the Miami Steamship Company, Nassau, Bahamas for £3,000 but company went into liquidation, and vessel resold for £2,750 to Turners and Hickman, brokers, for further service.
1927: Sold to the Bahamas Shipping Co. Ltd., Nassau.
1928: Sold to the Florida Inter-Island Steamship Co. Ltd., Nassau
1929: Renamed CITY OF NASSAU.
1937: Broken up during second quarter.

4. WALMER 1923-1935
O.N. 95358 518g 211n.
195.0 x 28.1 x 14.3 feet.
Cargo capacity: 22,543 cubic feet.
Two x T.3-cyl. by Denny and Company, Dumbarton; 104 NHP, 1,400 IHP, 14 knots.
11.10.1894: Launched by William Denny and Brothers, Dumbarton (Yard No. 501).
30.11.1894: Delivered at a cost of £17,600, which included her sister CALVADOS.
12.12.1894: Registered in the ownership of the London, Brighton and South Coast Railway Company, London as TROUVILLE.
3.10.1901: Sold to the South Eastern and Chatham Railway Companies' Managing Committee, London for £11,500.
29.10.1901: Renamed WALMER.
1.1.1923: Transferred to the Southern Railway Company, London for Strait of Dover services.
15.7.1925: Stem and plates damaged in collision with the Dover pier on arrival from Boulogne.
18.5.1929: Collided with the quay at Calais as a result of defective quay lighting.
24.12.1929: Blown heavily on to the Calais quayside in a strong gale.
11.1935: Broken up at Hendrik-ido-Ambacht by N.V. Holland Scheepswerf.
1.11.1935: Register closed.

Laura in London and South Western Railway colours. *[Ian Boyle collection]*

5. ULRICA 1923-1928
O.N. 104961 383g 151n.
149.9 x 24.1 x 7.7 feet.
Cargo capacity: 18,723 cubic feet.
T. 3-cyl. by Muir and Houston, Glasgow; 75 NHP, 500 IHP, 11½ knots.
12.2.1895: Launched by the Ailsa Shipbuilding Company, Troon (Yard No. 49).
30.3.1895: Registered in the ownership of the Trustees of the Congested Districts Board of Ireland, Dublin as GRANUAILE.
31.3.1915: Sold to Peter Morrison, Glasgow.
21.2.1916: Sold to R.E.V. James Ltd., Southampton
18.7.1916: Sold to the London and South Western Railway Company, London for £10,430.
12.9.1916: Renamed ULRICA.
1.1.1923: Transferred to the Southern Railway Company, London.
9.3.1923: Seriously damaged when stranded on rocks off Guernsey after a marker buoy had washed away.
19.9.1925: Damaged French steamer SAINT-BRIEUC (461/1904) at Jersey.
20.6.1928: Register closed on sale to T.C. Par, Netherlands for £700 for breaking up.

6. DEAL 1923-1926
O.N. 95360 572g 240n.
195.0 x 28.1 x 14.3 feet.
Cargo capacity 21,940 cubic feet.
Two x T.3-cyl. by Denny and Company, Dumbarton; 104 NHP, 15 knots.
9.5.1896: Launched by William Denny and Brothers, Dumbarton (Yard No. 534).
11.7.1896: Delivered at a cost of £20,296.
21.7.1896: Registered in the ownership of the London, Brighton and South Coast Railway Company, London as PRINCE ARTHUR.
2.10.1901: Sold to the South Eastern and Chatham Railway Companies' Managing Committee, London.
29.10.1901: Renamed DEAL.
1.1.1923: Transferred to the Southern Railway for Strait of Dover services.

23.2.1926: Sold to Thomas Young, Sunderland for £1,750 for breaking up.
3.5.1926: Register closed.

7. MAIDSTONE 1923-1925
O.N. 110092 539g 221n.
195.0 x 28.1 x 14.2 feet.
Cargo capacity: 28,370 cubic feet.
T.3-cyl. by Denny and Company, Dumbarton; 52 NHP, 11·6 knots
15.3.1899: Launched by William Denny and Brothers, Dumbarton (Yard No. 609).
5.4.1899: Delivered at a cost of £16,202.
6.4.1899: Registered in the ownership of the London, Chatham and Dover Railway Company, London as MAIDSTONE.
10.7.1900: Transferred to the South Eastern and Chatham Railway Companies' Managing Committee, London.
1.1.1923: Transferred to the Southern Railway Company, London for Strait of Dover services.
1925: Sold to Stanlee Shipbreaking for £1,800 for breaking up.
14.8.1925: Register closed.

Maidstone. [Ian Boyle collection]

8. CANTERBURY 1923-1926

O.N. 112803 561g 144n.
204.2 (195.4) x 28.0 x 14.3 feet.
Cargo capacity 19,780 cubic feet.
Two x T.3-cyl. by Denny and Company,
Dumbarton; 104 NHP, 15·5 knots.
6.12.1900: Launched by William Denny and
Brothers, Dumbarton (Yard No. 640).
25.1.1901: Delivered at a cost of £26,049.
26.1.1901: Registered in the ownership of
the South Eastern and Chatham Railway
Companies Managing Committee, London
1.1.1923: Transferred to the Southern
Railway Company, London for Strait of
Dover services.
24.6.1926: Sold to Walter E. Guinness,
London for £3,500 for conversion to a yacht.
23.9.1926: Renamed ARPHA.
7.2.1938: Sold to the Crete Shipping Co.
Ltd. (John A. Leighton, manager), London.
21.6.1938: Transferred to Sark Motor Ships
Ltd., Guernsey (John A. Leighton, London,
manager) and refitted for commercial
passenger service.
5.11.1939: Requisition by the Admiralty as
an armed boarding vessel until 7.1.1946.
17.1.1946: Sold to The Shell Company of
Venezuela Ltd. (Anglo-Saxon Petroleum Co.
Ltd.), London.
11.6.1946: Register closed on sale to the
Caribbean Petroleum Co. Ltd., Maracaibo,
Venezuela and renamed CORIANO.
1951: Sold to J.M. Pérez Hernández,
Venezuela.
1955: Sold to North American Smelting
Company, Wilmington, Delaware, U.S.A.
28.10.55: Arrived at Bordentown, New
Jersey, U.S.A. and subsequently broken up.

9. RINA 1923-1926

O.N. 113673 548g 227n.
170.0 x 27.1 x 11.4 feet.
Cargo capacity: 28,800 cubic feet.
T. 3-cyl. by Bow, McLachlan and Co. Ltd.,
Paisley; 69 NHP, 500 IHP, 9½ knots.
28.12.1901: Launched by the Ardrossan Dry
Dock and Shipbuilding Co. Ltd., Ardrossan
(Yard No. 186).
17.3.1902: Registered in the ownership
of R.H. Penney and Sons, Shoreham as
ALGETHI.
21.6.1922: Sold to James Mordan, Paris.
5.10.1922: Renamed RINA.
7.10.1922: Sold to the London and South
Western Railway Company, London for
£9,083.
1.1.1923: Transferred to the Southern
Railway Company, London.
25.2.1926: Sold to the York Line Ltd.
(Richards, Longstaff and Co. Ltd.,
managers), London for £1,250.
1.3.1926: Sold to the Striver Steamship Co.
Ltd. (H. Harrison, manager), London.
3.1926: Sold to G. Dormio fu Z., Bari, Italy
and renamed COSTANZA.
1930: Owners became Ditta Giuseppe
Dormio, Bari.
By 1941: Sold to Alfino e figli, Catania, Italy.
14.10.1940: Requisitioned by the Italian
Navy as an auxiliary.

After serving 25 years as a Strait of Dover cargo steamer, *Canterbury* (upper) was renamed *Arpha*, firstly as a private yacht, then, as shown here (lower), as an excursion vessel. *[Both A.M.S. Russell collection]*

23.8.1941: Sunk by air attack 36 miles east
of Lampedusa whilst on a voyage from
Lampedusa to Tripoli.

10. VENA 1923-1928

O.N. 113640 565g 229n.
170.4 x 27.2 x 11.4 feet.
Cargo capacity: 29,677 cubic feet.
T. 3-cyl. by Ross and Duncan, Govan; 81
NHP, 500 IHP, 10 knots.
12.4.1902: Launched by Scott and Sons,
Bowling (Yard No. 151).
13.5.1902: Registered in the ownership of
Joseph Rank Ltd., Hull as CLARENCE.
5.1902: Completed.
13.2.1907: Sold to R.H. Penney and Sons,
Shoreham.
13.3.1907: Renamed ALGEIBA.
21.6.1922: Sold to James Mordan, Paris, but
retained British registration.
5.10.1922: Renamed VENA
7.10.1922: Sold to the London and South
Western Railway Company, London for
£9,083.
1.1.1923: Transferred to the Southern
Railway Company, London for Southampton
services.
18.2.1926: Sold to the York Line Ltd.
(Richards, Longstaff and Co. Ltd.,

managers), London for £2,400.
23.2.1926: Sold to Wilson and Reid Ltd.
(Thomas Wilson, manager), Belfast.
11.1928: Sold to V. and S. Castella,
Casablanca, Morocco and renamed RABAT.
1953: Broken up.

11. FOLKESTONE 1923-1926

O.N. 118353 496g 100n.
192.2 x 28.1 x14.3 feet.
Cargo capacity 19,990 cubic feet.
Two x T.3-cyl. by Denny and Company,
Dumbarton; 104 NHP, 15·5 knots.
13.10.1903: Launched by William Denny
and Brothers, Dumbarton (Yard No. 703).
26.11.1903: Registered in the ownership
of the South Eastern and Chatham Railway
Companies' Managing Committee, London
as FOLKESTONE.
3.12.1903: Delivered at a cost of £22,500.
10.1914: Requisitioned by the Admiralty as
a minesweeper until 1.1920.
1.1.1923: Transferred to the Southern
Railway Company, London for Strait of
Dover services.
30.8.1923: Rescued five French seamen whose
vessel had foundered in heavy seas in the
Channel whilst on passage to Boulogne.
25.11.1926: Sold to Major Henry Keswick,

Dumfries for £6,800 for conversion to a yacht.
28.2.1927: Renamed SOLWAY.
31.3.1930: Register closed on sale to United
States subjects and renamed BWANA.
25.9.1930: Registered in the ownership of
Sidney R. Berry, Southampton.
29.11.1930: Sold to Sir Alexander H.
Maguire, London.
20.2.1935: Sold to Pollock Brown and Co.
Ltd. and probably broken up at Northam,
Southampton
8.6.1936: Register closed.

12. ADA 1923-1934
O.N. 119709 489g 198n.
175.3 x 28.1 x 12.4 feet.
Cargo capacity 25,050 cubic feet.
T. 3-cyl. by Gourlay Brothers and Co.
(Dundee) Ltd., Dundee; 93 NHP, 1,000 IHP,
12 knots.
4.4.1905: Launched by Gourlay Brothers
and Co. (Dundee) Ltd., Dundee (Yard No.
216).
25.4.1905: Registered in the ownership of
the London and South Western Railway
Company, London as ADA. She cost
£13,200.
1.1.1923: Transferred to the Southern
Railway Company, London for Southampton
services:
3.1934: Sold to The Darwen and Mostyn
Iron Company for £750 for breaking up at
Mostyn, Flintshire.
25.10.1934: Register closed.

13. BERTHA 1923-1940
O.N. 119725 528g 139n
175.3 feet x 28.1 x 12.5 feet
Cargo capacity 22,300 cubic feet.
T. 3-cyl. by Gourlay Brothers and Co.
(Dundee) Ltd., Dundee; 93 NHP, 1,000 IHP,
11 knots.
9.11.1905: Launched by Gourlay Brothers
and Co. (Dundee) Ltd., Dundee (Yard No.
219).
1.12.1905: Registered in the ownership of
the London and South Western Railway
Company, London as BERTHA. She cost
£13,900.
1.1.1923: Transferred to the Southern
Railway Company, London for Southampton
services:

A stern view of the 1903 cargo steamer *Folkestone* alongside the pier at her namesake port, with a railway paddle steamer, probably *Princess of Wales*, berthed beyond her. *[A.M.S. Russell collection]*

16.1.1923: Damaged in collision with the
corner of berths 6 and 7 at Southampton.
10.12.1929: Collided with the tug ABEILLE
22 at Cherbourg.
9.11.1933: Sold to Metal Industries Ltd.,
Glasgow, for £1,400 for use as a salvage
vessel.
1.5.1940: Register closed on purchase by the
Admiralty, London.
19.4.1947: Registered in the ownership
of Risdon Beazley Ltd. (R.A. Beazley,
manager), Southampton as TOPMAST No. 6.
8.1948: Sold to S.A. des Produits
Metallurgiques 'SAPROMET', Antwerp,
Belgium and broken up
23.8.1948: Register closed.

14. BRITTANY/ALDERSHOT 1923-1933
O.N. 105657 618g 252n.
192.0 x 29.2 x 14.2 feet.
Cargo capacity 29,860 cubic feet.
T. 3-cyl. by Earle's Shipbuilding and
Engineering Co. Ltd., Hull; 82 NHP, 900
IHP, 12½ knots.
9.7.1910: Launched by Earle's Shipbuilding
and Engineering Co. Ltd., Hull (Yard No. 572).

25.8.1910: Registered in the ownership
of the London, Brighton and South Coast
Railway Company, London as BRITTANY.
30.5.1912: Sold to the London and South
Western Railway Company, London for
£15,261.
1.1.1923: Transferred to the Southern
Railway Company, London for Southampton
services.
8.7.1926: Shafting snapped during a
crossing to Le Havre
10.7.1926: Returned to Southampton in tow.
5.11.1929: Stem damaged against the pier
on entering Jersey in exceptional weather.
4.4.1933: Renamed ALDERSHOT.
6.1.1937: Register closed on sale to D.
Tripcovich & Ci. Società Anonima di
Navigazione, Rimorchi e Salvataggi, Trieste,
Italy for £2,350 for conversion to a salvage
vessel and renamed HERCULES.
24.11.1941: Torpedoed and sunk by HMS
TRIUMPH in Heraklion harbour, Crete,
while engaged in salvaging the German
steamer NORBURG (2,392/1922) which
had been torpedoed and sunk off Candia
12.9.1941.

John de S. Winser, 1934-2014

We are sorry to report that John Winser died earlier this year. The above and a further forthcoming article had been accepted before his death and are published with the kind permission of his family.

John's particular maritime interest was short-sea shipping, a passion stimulated by a chance sighting of the cross-channel steamer *Falaise* during a childhood holiday in Jersey. This interest was reflected in his six published books and over 70 magazine articles, the involvement of short-sea and coastal shipping in wartime operations being a particular fascination. His published work was characterised by diligent research and immaculate attention to detail (as those correspondents who challenged his work discovered).

However, John was also an enthusiast for other forms of transport, including the Avro Lancaster and Vulcan bombers, as well as steam trains. In addition he had a love of the bands of the Royal Marines (although he admitted that during his national service with the Royal Artillery he did not prove to be a natural soldier) and was an active supporter of the RNLI.

Professionally, John was involved in the travel industry. This included the meticulous logging of worldwide shipping movements for P&O and, prior to his retirement, the role of managing director of a specialist international tour operator. His family fondly remember that holidays were planned with the same precision as the tours he organised professionally, even down to every participant being provided with an itinerary.

John will be much missed, and not only by editors who were grateful for his well-presented and totally trustworthy typescripts. Our sympathies go to John's daughters, Juliette, Katherine and Helen, who are thanked for their help in compiling this brief obituary.

It is tempting to place this photograph of *Scandinavia* (right) in conjunction with one of, say *British Pride* (160,216/2000), and comment on how the British Petroleum fleet has changed. Tempting, but hazardous. As very much children of the steam and motor ship age, your editors rely on examining funnel markings to confirm that a particular ship is correctly identified, and they flounder when a vessel like this has no more than a stovepipe. But assuming this *is* the 461gt *Scandinavia* built by N.V. Werf V. Rijkee & Company, of Rotterdam in 1905, she was indeed owned for ten years by various antecedents or associates of the oil company. The three-masted steel schooner was built for William H. Muller & Company, Rotterdam, and fitted with a paraffin engine. In 1912 she passed to British Petroleum Co. Ltd. without change of name, but underwent several transfers before ending up with the British Tanker Co. Ltd. On 20th October 1922 she was wrecked on Portland breakwater whilst on a voyage from London to Manchester. The interest of this vessel, not illustrated in any of several histories of BP, excuses what appears to be a cracked negative from which the print was taken.

The delightful photograph below depicts the 1859, Scotts of Greenock-

built *Le Gouet* (the photographer labelled the negative 'Le Quoet'). Confirmation of her identity comes from a rather indistinct photograph of her under her former name *Rebecca*, reproduced the editor's 'Cambrian Coasters'. For much of her long career she was owned by the Carnarvonshire and Merionethshire Steamship Co. Ltd. which maintained weekly sailings between its home in Porthmadog and Liverpool, using *Rebecca* from 1864 to 1896. The photograph dates from between April 1904, when as *Le Gouet* the old iron steamer was bought by Vicomte le Guales de Mezaubran of Legue, France, and 4th November 1907 when she was wrecked near Ile d'Oleron whilst carrying a cargo of oats from Morlaix to Bordeaux.

CHELWOOD TO CHELWOOD: 60 YEARS OF COLLIERS
John Lingwood

During the nineteenth and twentieth centuries, three companies dominated what had become known as the North East Coast coal trade: William France, Fenwick; Stephenson, Clarke and William Cory. Each built up substantial fleets of colliers to serve not only their own customers, but to operate on long-term charter to the gas and electricity undertakings in the south of England, some of which in the course of time would go on to establish their own fleets (but with ship management in the hands of one or other of the giants). The decision of France, Fenwick to build a raised quarter deck collier of about 4,000 tons deadweight capacity with machinery aft, the design of which addressed, and largely overcame, the problems which had previously restricted vessels of this type to about 2,500 tons capacity, produced a prototype which was to be further developed to serve as the standard collier in this vital trade for almost sixty years. Built by S.P. Austin and Sons at their Wear Dockyard, Sunderland, the new vessel was delivered in 1928 and given the name *Chelwood* and its design was described and illustrated in an article published in 'Record' 54.

Preparations for war
The 1930s were overshadowed by war clouds and reference is also made in the previous article to moves put in hand by British Government departments, who were mindful of the devastating losses resulting from the reintroduction by Germany in 1917 of an unrestricted submarine warfare campaign, to prepare a portfolio of designs of the various types of cargo vessel most likely to be required in an emergency, so that construction of replacement tonnage could be quickly put in hand if war was declared. By 1939 the *Chelwood* design had been sufficiently developed, with improvements in propelling machinery and equipment, to be included in that portfolio as the standard 4,100-ton deadweight collier, to be built primarily for service in the vital North East Coast coal trade.

The German Navy's attacks on Allied shipping in the First World War, and particularly following the 1917 change in tactics, eventually came close to bringing about a totally different end to the conflict. This possibility was only countered once a convoy system designed to protect the main supply lines was successfully introduced. As a

A reminder of how the *Chelwood* of 1928 appeared. In contrast to the photographs in 'Record' 54, this image dates from before the Second World War, and the collier lacks the accommodation for DEMS gunners which was fitted abaft her funnel during the war. *[Laurence Dunn]*

consequence, as early as 1935 plans began to be laid for a similar system to be put in place if a second conflict materialised. The sinking of the unescorted liner *Athenia* on the 3rd September 1939 with the loss of 112 lives initiated these arrangements, and on the 6th September the first UK convoy set sail. Indicative perhaps of the importance placed on the need to keep the North East Coast coal supply line to the south open, it was on this route that the earliest convoys operated and in total 1,840 FS (Forth to Southend) convoys were run between 1939 and 1945.

The equivalent northbound FN convoy operated on 1,744 occasions escorting 50,275 vessels with 54,517 having sailed in the corresponding southward voyages. However, a sobering thought is that, despite the efforts of the escorts, some 200 vessels were lost on the coast mainly from enemy action. Sadly, this total included the first North Sea loss of the war, occurring just seven days after the declaration when William France, Fenwick's *Goodwood* (an almost brand new *Chelwood* type considered by its owner to be the best in the trade at the time, fitted as she was with the latest North Eastern Marine triple expansion machinery), sailing in an FS convoy, was sunk just hours after leaving port with a full cargo of coal for Bayonne. Her owner's official history suggests that she was torpedoed by a submarine which was itself later destroyed by the convoy escorts. However, official and other publications listing war losses maintain

that she was mined, and the submarine *U 9* has since been identified as the craft that laid the mine, four days earlier on 6th September.

Of course not all the vessels sailing in these convoys were colliers but the numbers do give an indication of the extent of this vital trade. Although eventually most deep-sea cargo vessels arriving from overseas were handled in West Coast ports some (especially in early days of the war) were of necessity directed via the north of Scotland to east coast destinations and would be included in FS/FN convoy statistics.

Cory and Stephenson Clarke
As described in 'Record' 54, although William France, Fenwick continued to add *Chelwood* type vessels to their fleet during the 1930s, the other principal operators in the North East trade, Stephenson Clarke (and their managed public utilities fleets) plus William Cory concentrated on building smaller vessels to serve their own extensive domestic and industrial customers in the southern counties, which also included a number of gas and electricity undertakings. Much of this coal came from Yorkshire collieries and was loaded at Goole, and ship dimensions had to comply with port restrictions there as well as at the discharging ports. Nevertheless these smaller vessels were easily recognized as scaled-down versions of their larger sisters. Ten 2,700-ton deadweight vessels which William Cory built between 1934 and 1944 were typical. Their significance

to this narrative is that it was one of this series, *Corfen,* completed in 1940, which was the first North East Coast collier to be fitted with MacGregor steel hatch covers (the *Chelwood* type not receiving its first examples until 1942). It is noteworthy that the designs of some of these smaller vessels were also included in the portfolio of wartime standard vessels.

Cory's business also included trade with the continent for which they employed larger, usually engines-midships colliers. However, in 1929 they decided to see what benefits this new, engines-aft design offered, and took delivery of *Corglen,* a 4,310-ton deadweight vessel from the Cowpen Drydock and Shipbuilding Co. Ltd., Blyth and four years later of *Corhampton,* a 3,800-ton deadweight sister of *Chelwood* from Austins. Because their trading pattern often required different grades of coal to be carried in one shipment, this vessel was configured with five holds rather than four as adopted by France, Fenwick. In 1936 Cory's finally adopted the engines aft, raised quarter deck design as standard for their larger colliers, many of which were built by the Burntisland Shipbuilding Co. Ltd. with most retaining the five-hold arrangement.

Between 1915 and 1928 a series of business developments involving Stephenson Clarke included the formation of a new subsidiary, the Normandy Shipping Co. Ltd., mainly to carry duff (virtually powdered) coal from north of England and South Wales coal fields to supply the patent fuel works in France owned by the Welsh coal mining and exporting group Powell Duffryn. Between 1916 and 1925 when this venture was disposed of, a fleet of 11 new and second hand vessels was acquired for this purpose. Changes in the management of the original Stephenson Clarke partnership during this period culminated in 1928

Cory's *Corglen* of 1929 in a post-war view: note the radar and a possible 'bandstand' aft for wartime defensive armament. Sold in 1955, she had various, mostly Greek, further owners who put her under free flags as first *Michael A* and later *Capetan Andreas.* She was scrapped at El Ferrol in April 1966. *[Roy Fenton collection]*

when Powell Duffryn acquired the entire share capital of the company which now traded as Stephenson Clarke and Associated Companies Ltd.

Even before this total merger the two companies had in 1920 strengthened their 1915 association by each taking a 45% holding in another new company, the Maris Export and Trading Co. Ltd. This was formed to combine their respective extensive North East Coast/South Wales export activities, and it was for this company and not their own account that Stephenson Clarke placed their first order for a large, engines-aft, raised-quarter-deck collier. Given the name *Ilse,* when delivered in 1929 by Smith's Dock Co. Ltd., South Bank, Middlesbrough, her deadweight of 4,300 tons and principal dimensions were similar to those of *Chelwood,* and to a series of slightly larger vessels completed a few years earlier by Smith's Dock for the French PLM/SNA railway operation (see 'Record' 17 and 18).

Destined initially for the Hamburg trade, *Ilse* was strengthened for navigation in ice. However, in 1936 she was transferred to the parent company's fleet, only to suffer the fate of many East Coast colliers when sunk off Cromer during an E-boat attack in October 1942.

Gas industry colliers

With much of its business centred on serving the smaller Channel ports and Thames-side wharves, Stephenson Clarke had rarely needed to add vessels larger than 2,500 deadweight tons to its fleet and their 1920s and 1930s new buildings were mainly of that size. However, in May and October 1936 they did take delivery from S.P. Austin of two vessels based on the *Chelwood* model, but not for their own account. Since 1911 the company had managed the collier fleet of the Gas, Light and Coke Company which supplied gas to most of London north of the Thames. Coal was delivered either to their extensive riverside Beckton gas works at Gallions Reach, when opened in 1870 being one of the largest in the world, or to the mechanised discharging jetty in Regent's Canal Dock at Limehouse, with gas works further up-river or inaccessible to sea going vessels receiving coal transhipped from there by lighter or canal craft (see the photograph of the dock and accompanying article in 'Record' 49). Eventually it become possible to send larger, improved design, so-called 'flat iron' (low air draft) colliers further up the Thames and new buildings of this special type began to predominate amongst the ships delivered into the gas company fleets and similarly into those of the electricity generating undertakings with power stations higher on the Thames.

Ilse of 1929 in Stephenson, Clarke's colours. *[Ships in Focus]*

Mr Therm of 1935, now owned by the Gas, Light and Coke Company's successor, the North Thames Gas Board. She had a satisfyingly long career, arrived at Dunston-on-Tyne for breaking up by Clayton and Davie Ltd. in April 1959. *[F.R. Sherlock]*

The new vessels, given the names *Mr. Therm* and *Gasfire*, were the largest 'Chelwoods' yet built with dimensions of 329.0 x 45 .7 x 20.0 feet and a deadweight of some 4,600 tons. Dispensing with the large midships water ballast tank of the basis design gave a cargo capacity of almost 210,000 cubic feet, allowing a full cargo of relatively light Durham gas coal stowing at around 50 cubic feet to the ton to be loaded for Beckton. *Gasfire* was unfortunate to have her stern blown off in an E-boat attack in October 1940 but was salved and returned to her builder for repairs which were completed on the 3rd May1941. Just seven weeks later, however, she struck a mine off the Suffolk coast and was lost. *Mr. Therm* was more fortunate and continued to serve Beckton until 1959, with a break for the D-day operations for which she was modified by having large openings cut in the bulkheads dividing her holds to allow tanks and other heavy equipment to be loaded more easily.

Corys upgrade
Turning to the William Cory fleet, some of its larger units now needed to be replaced, and also in 1936 it was decided to place an order with Scottish east coast builder Burntisland Shipbuilding Co. Ltd. for a 4,380-ton deadweight, engines-aft collier with dimensions of 308 x 44.5t x 19.7 feet and a gross tonnage of 2,841 and, therefore, similar to the Austin's design. Named *Cormount*, this vessel was followed into service in 1939 by two sisters, the trio – all of which were to be

war losses – becoming the basis design for the company's future large colliers. The Burntisland company had been formed, just as the First World War was ending, by two Tyneside brothers Wilfred and Amos Ayre, who together played leading roles in British shipbuilding industry developments in both world wars and for most of the first half of the twentieth century. The yard quickly gained success building cargo vessels of varying sizes and types, including many which subsequently saw service in the North East Coast coal trade, in particular a succession of up-river, 'flat iron' colliers for the London utility companies.

A sister to *Cormount* delivered to the Polish company Polskarob in 1938 was *Robur VIII*, and a history of this basically coal mining concern and its small fleet of colliers can be found in 'Record' 13 where it is noted that had it not been for the outbreak of the Second World War, *Robur VIII* would have become the forerunner of a series of sister ships built for the company. Most of their vessels managed to escape from Poland as the German army invaded and were subsequently involved in the North East coal trade, interestingly managed by William Cory. However, *Robur VIII*, operating under the Free Polish name

Cormount of 1936 and her two 1939-built sisters, *Cormarsh* and *Cormead*, were mined or sunk by E-boats, but Cory were allowed to return to Burntisland for replacements, including the slightly enlarged *Cormain* of 1942. Renamed *Coldridge* for Coastwise Colliers Ltd. between 1946 and 1949, she reverted to *Cormain*, serving until 1969 when she was converted to a barge. *[Roy Fenton collection]*

A typical engines-amidships collier, *Zelo* of 1921 was owned by the Pelton Steamship Co. Ltd. of Newcastle, and had been built by S.P. Austin and Sons Ltd. at Sunderland. She steamed on in the North East coal trade until 1955, when Greek owners renamed her first *Kyriakoula* and later *Pitsa*. She was demolished at Perama in 1965. *[Roy Fenton collection]*

Zagloba, became a war loss much further afield whilst sailing in a convoy from New York to Manchester.

Smaller collier companies

Mention should be made that, as well as the big three, there were other, smaller companies, working on a less regular basis in the North East Coast coal trade to the south of England and to the Continent, and also running northward to serve Scottish customers, particularly owners of large trawler fleets. Very few of these vessels exceeded 2,000-tons deadweight mark and most which did were engines-midship type of around 4,500 tons deadweight, built in the 1920s and owned by companies associated with the Northumberland and Durham coal mining groups who usually had ships available, especially in winter months, to meet the demand for additional tonnage for the London and South Coast utilities.

In 1930, as described in 'Record' 54, Austins booked their first order for a *Chelwood* type collier from one of these smaller companies, delivering the 4,300-ton deadweight *Harraton* to the Tanfield Steamship Co. Ltd. of Newcastle, part of the extensive Lambton, Hetton and Joicey Collieries coal mining group. The following year the similar-sized, engines-aft *Beneficient* was delivered by the Sunderland shipyard of William Pickersgill and Sons Ltd. to the local Westoll Steamships Ltd. The connection here being that although senior members of both the Austin and Pickersgill families were still active in their respective shipyards, both shipbuilding companies were actually owned by the Westoll family, once arguably the largest ship owner in Sunderland with a deep-sea fleet which particularly took coal to Mediterranean and Black Sea ports and returned with grain, as well as working in the North East Coast and continental coal trades, and the contract may well have been transferred to the Pickersgill yard in order to keep it open in what were very difficult times. *Beneficient* was to help keep the Thames supply line open until becoming a war loss in 1940.

Westoll's *Beneficient* was another mine victim whilst in the North East coast coal trade. On 17th December 1940 she was sunk off Southend whilst on a voyage from Sunderland to London with a cargo of coal. Note the derricks, indicating that she regularly worked outside the coastal coal trade, to ports where shoreside cargo handling gear could not be guaranteed. *[Ships in Focus]*

The short-lived *Goodwood*. Completed in August 1937, on 10th September 1939 she was mined and sunk one mile south east of Flamborough Head whilst on a voyage from the Tyne to Bayonne with a cargo of coal. *[Nautical Photo Agency/Roy Fenton collection]*

With *Mr. Therm* and *Gasfire* successfully delivered, Austin's order book for the last few years of the 1930s was filled with a mix of 'flat iron' colliers for the Gas, Light and Coke and London Power companies and smaller vessels for Stephenson Clarke and Cory. William France, Fenwick ordered a vessel of 1,600 tons deadweight for their Goole/London general cargo trade, a 2,400-ton version of *Chelwood* for the London coal trade, and the unfortunate *Goodwood,* sunk as noted just one week after war was declared. One month later, Austins launched the similar *Lea Grange* as a replacement for *Harraton* which had recently been sold to French owners, making her the last of the pre-war *Chelwoods*. Already the wartime emergency plans had been actioned: convoys were operating and newly-formed government departments

had taken control of shipbuilding, marine engine building, ship repairing and ship operation, with the building of new ships in accordance with the portfolio of standard designs ready to commence as soon as shipyards had cleared the backlog of existing orders. The standard large collier based on the updated *Chelwood* design was 321.9 feet overall, 311.4 feet between perpendiculars, 44.5 feet beam and 19.3 feet depth. Deadweight was about 4,100 tons and gross tonnage 2,800/2,900 tons. Powered by a triple-expansion steam engine of around 1,075 BHP, service speed was between 9½ and 10½ knots.

Wartime collier replacements
In order to maintain the numerical strength of their fleets, the gas and electricity undertakings and the owners

operating ships on charter to these companies were allowed to replace war losses by ordering vessels privately and to give them traditional company names. Austin's output throughout the war consisted almost entirely of this type of vessel, with significant numbers also built by the Burntisland company. Modifications made to the design to suit wartime requirements were, in the main, economies in the amount of steel and other materials used in construction, provision of defensive armament and additional accommodation for the DEMS personnel carried to man this, usually solved by building a small deckhouse on the aft end of the boat deck. However, in 1943 with preparations for the invasion of France beginning to be considered, some more significant changes were made. William France, Fenwick's newbuilding *Wrenwood,* for instance, had additional hull strength and heavy-lift cargo gear added so that tanks and other heavy military equipment might be carried. It is interesting to note that the profile sketch of the design included (page 206) in the second edition of Sawyer and Mitchell's 'The Empire Ships' seems to suggest that the vessels were laid out with only two cargo holds but a more detailed builder's general arrangement plan included in MacRae and Waine's 'The Steam Collier Fleets' illustrates a four hold vessel.

Also included in the standard ship portfolio was a design for a smaller, intermediate class collier with the choice again falling on an Austins-built vessel. *Icemaid* had been completed in 1936 to

Another Austin product, the *Wrenwood* retained her heavy wartime masts post-war, although her derricks had gone. Renamed *Collingbourne* for transfer to Coastwise Colliers in 1946, she was back as *Wrenwood* in 1949. Ten years on, she became *Ethel C* for a Greek owner, but sank after her cargo of scrap iron shifted off the East Coast of the USA in April 1960. *[World Ship Society Ltd.]*

148

Icemaid awaits a coal cargo in the Tyne, with a Royal Navy frigate in the background. Even colliers like her, which were intended to spend their lives shuttling between ports where cargo gear was completely irrelevant, had the facility to rig derricks: note the lower set of crosstrees. These would have come into their own when *Icemaid* was sold to Greek owners in 1958 to become *Papeira M*. Under this name a grounding at Mogadisciu in January 1963 left her a constructive total loss, although she was not sent to Spilt for demolition for almost three years. *[Ships in Focus]*

a scaled-down *Chelwood* configuration to serve the Regent's Canal transhipment installation of the Gas, Light and Coke Company, and with dimensions of 272 x 40 feet, four holds and hatches, a gross tonnage of 1,964 tons and a deadweight of around 2,825 tons, a total of 26 were built during the war. These contracts were placed on behalf of the Ministry of War Transport and allocated to private ship owners for management, all bearing *Empire* names when launched.

In 1940 the Admiralty also introduced another series of 4,100 tons deadweight vessels, similar to the standard colliers building by Austin and Burntisland but intended for a wider range of cargoes, ordering what eventually became nine vessels from West Hartlepool builder, William Gray. These were also delivered to the Ministry of War Transport, given 'Empire' names and allocated to private owners for management. Two were operated on the North East Coast by William France, Fenwick for a short period, eliciting

the comment in that company's official history that they were of 'much the same design as we had been developing (e.g. *Chelwood* derivatives) but not up to our standard'! After the war only one of these, *Empire Gower,* became a regular in the north east coast trade, becoming *Rogate* in Stephenson Clarke's fleet, although two more sailed as *Holmside* and *Gripfast* for two independent Newcastle-based companies who occasionally chartered their vessels to the London utilities.

Built in 1941 as *Empire Brook*, one of a group of 4,100-ton deadweight colliers from William Gray and Co. Ltd., *Gripfast* was owned by the Newbiggin Steamship Co. Ltd. from 1948 to 1960. After a succession of Greek owners, she sank off Socotra Island, Sri Lanka, in December 1967. *[Ships in Focus]*

Peacetime changes

The ending of the Second World War in 1945 was quickly followed by the termination of the Admiralty emergency shipbuilding programmes and the implementation of plans for the disposal of those vessels built under these, and nominally owned by the Ministry of War Transport. The 'Icemaids' and Gray's 4,100-ton deadweight colliers were amongst those made available to private owners, many of whom had been their managers during the war. Austin, Burntisland and their recently acquired subsidiary Hall, Russell of Aberdeen, continued to build peacetime versions of the wartime 4,100 ton design with the Sunderland company's first post-war delivery in January 1946 introducing a new owner to the type. The South Metropolitan Gas Company, serving South East London, used its own ships to supply their 1881-built gas works at East Greenwich and during the war had lost four of its fleet of seven ageing 2,500 tons deadweight colliers. Their new *Effra* resulted from a complete change in their fuel supply policy which now required larger shipments. Two years later demand necessitated a second vessel, satisfied when *Catford* was delivered from the Wear Dockyard, becoming the first diesel-engined *Chelwood* when fitted with Ruston and Hornsby propulsion machinery.

Effra was completed in January 1946 for the South Metropolitan Gas Company, and was photographed in their colours sometime before the funnel design of their successors, the South Eastern Gas Board, was substituted in 1949. Sold in 1967, she served Greek owners as *Yannakis Fanis* and *Giulia* before arriving at Split in April 1974 to be broken up. *[Roy Fenton collection]*

In March 1946 Stephenson Clarke, William France, Fenwick, and Cory jointly formed a new company, Coastwise Colliers Ltd., to charter vessels to the independent County of London Electricity Supply Co. Ltd. which operated its own Thames-side power stations. Vessels were transferred from their own fleets to get the new firm started with Coastwise then taking delivery in April 1948 and February 1949 of two new buildings from Austins, *Coleford* and *Colville*. They and the transferred vessels were later returned to the partners when it was decided to wind up Coastwise Colliers following the nationalisation of the electricity undertakings. At the same time Coastwise also ordered ten 1,700 tons deadweight colliers (small *Chelwoods*) to take coal from Goole to power stations along the south and south west coasts.

Peacetime had brought its own problems for the collier-owning companies on the North East Coast. War losses had to be replaced and long overdue repairs and surveys carried out on the surviving vessels. The coal export market had all but disappeared, although partially compensating for this loss were the demands of a British market struggling to rebuild the home economy. The election of a Labour Government and the consequent nationalisation of the coal,

Colville was delivered to Coastwise Colliers Ltd. in February 1949, but within months this company was wound up and she was transferred to Stephenson Clarke Ltd. to become *Heyshott*. She steamed on until 1970 when, in April, Hughes Bolckow took delivery of her at their Blyth scrapyard. *[J. and M. Clarkson]*

This aerial view of *Hudson Deep* demonstrates that it was but a short step in design terms from the four-hatch collier to this prototype of the early bulk carrier. *Hudson Deep* worked in various deep-sea trades before being involved during 1963 in a series of successful trials of the feasibility of a 7,500-ton bulker working in the coastal coal trade. In 1972 she was sold to become *Irenes Hope* and in December 1978 she sank in the eastern Mediterranean after taking in water. *[Fotoflite incorporating Skyfotos]*

electricity and gas industries caused much rethinking by ship owners and the seeking of new markets. William France, Fenwick saw opportunities in the Canadian St. Lawrence River coal trade and in the West Indies sugar export business where producers were experimenting with the carriage of sugar in bulk, and in 1952 and 1953 they took delivery of two engines-aft, raised-quarter-deck vessels, essentially larger *Chelwoods* of around 7,800 tons deadweight from South Shields shipbuilder John Readhead for employment in these trades and ordered two similar vessels from William Pickersgill's Sunderland shipyard. However, the rapid changes in trading patterns at the time resulted in one of these contracts being converted to that for a 10,000-ton deadweight shelter-deck tramp.

The Hudson Steamship Co. Ltd. had been something of a fringe company in the North East Coast trade pre-war. Owned by London-based fuel distributors Samuel Williams, its colliers were mainly involved supplying that company's coal storage depot at Dagenham Dock, with occasional charters to the utilities. During the war they had been one of the owners allocated *Icemaid* type colliers for management and purchased two of these vessels when they were offered for sale. Later they ordered five new buildings from the Ailsa Shipbuilding

Company of Troon, including two of 4,500 tons deadweight, similar to the wartime standard but configured with five holds, and in 1949 they had fitted one of these for deep-sea trading resulting in its employment in the bulk sugar trade referred to above. The success of that charter led to them ordering *Hudson Deep* from Readheads in 1952, a 7,800-ton deadweight, diesel-engined sister to the William France, Fenwick pair. *Hudson Deep* was later to play an important role in the development of future colliers for what was then the Central Electricity Authority, when it was chartered to provide valuable experience regarding the feasibility of employing very much larger vessels to supply the London power stations.

Electricity colliers

But that decision was for the future. First we must go back to 1949/1950 when the recently formed nationalised British Electricity Authority (BEA) began putting in hand plans for restructuring the electricity generating industry. As far as the supply of coal by sea was concerned this initially included the acquisition of the ten 1,700-ton deadweight colliers ordered by Coastwise Colliers (see above) with management of these vessels now placed with Stephenson Clarke and Cory. To maintain the coal supply to new and/or modernised power stations particularly on

the Thames and at Ipswich and Brighton, contracts were placed for two new series of vessels. Ever since 1932, when the London Power Co. Ltd. first decided to build vessels to its own account with their management in the hands of Stephenson Clarke, the emphasis had been on building a sizeable fleet of 'flatiron' colliers to serve the Thames up-river power stations and only two conventional vessels of about 3,000 tons deadweight had been built which, supplemented by chartered tonnage, were used to satisfy the needs of generating plant such as that at Deptford in the lower reaches of the river.

The new building programme now implemented eventually embraced seven colliers of 4,600 tons deadweight mainly to serve the Thames and Ipswich, and four similar 3,700-ton vessels, built with slightly less beam in order to negotiate the locks at Shoreham and discharge at the Brighton power stations. All were basically a new generation of the *Chelwood* design but with an up-to-date specification including much improved crew accommodation. They were also suitable for loading and discharging at modernised facilities which, together with a slightly higher service speed, allowed for a faster turnround. Strangely, although most of Stephenson Clarke's own coaster fleet and the 'up river' fleet of what was now the Central Electricity Authority (CEA) which they managed, were fitted

First of 11 big colliers for the nationalised electricity industry, *Cliff Quay* was completed in 1950, and gave 33 years of service before being scrapped in Manchester in 1983. *[Ships in Focus]*

with diesel engines, these eleven vessels retained the time-honoured triple expansion main engine with the 4,600-ton deadweight series originally coal burning and only converted to oil fuel in the 1960s.

Building these vessels involved not only the originator of the *Chelwood* design S.P. Austin, but also William Pickersgill who were responsible for the design of the prototype of the series *Cliff Quay* and, following the merger of these two companies in 1954, Austin and Pickersgill, the Burntisland Shipbuilding Company and its subsidiary Hall, Russell. The CEA later invited private owners to build similar vessels for long-term charter, whilst in 1954 Stephenson Clarke, on behalf of the North Thames Gas Board, took delivery of the first of five almost identical versions of the 4,600-ton deadweight series to satisfy Beckton's requirements. Notably both Stephenson Clarke and William France, Fenwick – perhaps already thinking of the future – had ensured that one of each pair of this class of vessel which they ordered was equipped for deep-sea trading. In 1950 Stephenson Clarke had already taken delivery of the 4,800 tons deadweight motor collier *Minster,* lengthening her in 1964 to carry another 600 tons of cargo, and in 1959 another motor vessel, the 5,800 deadweight ton *Storrington* was added to a fleet which was also beginning to include new and second hand vessels of various sizes including four deep-sea tramp ships suitable for international general cargo trades. A relatively short-term venture into coastal tanker operation was also embarked upon. William France, Fenwick's involvement in the West Indies sugar and Canadian coal trades has already being noted whilst William

Cory sought alternative outlets in the oil tanker and ore carrier business.

End game

The end of the North East Coast coal trade was now clearly in sight with the electricity generating industry switching much of its fuel requirement to oil, and North Sea gas replacing coal gas as a source of domestic and industrial heating. Coal could be imported from overseas more cheaply than from British coal mines and, although some employment was found for the traditional colliers transhipping foreign coal discharged at continental ports, disposal of surplus tonnage became inevitable. The electricity industry was now trading as the Central Electricity Generating Board and in 1958 it announced that it was halving its fleet of over 50 vessels. Burntisland and its subsidiary Hall Russell at Aberdeen

(acquired in 1942), delivered their last *Chelwood* related colliers in the mid-fifties; the Fife yard's last two vessels of the type being the motor vessels *Corstar* and *Corsea* built for Cory and arranged with five cargo holds.

S.P. Austin, who had been responsible along with William, France Fenwick for the development of this successful design of a raised quarter deck/engines aft collier of about 4,000 tons deadweight in 1928, was now trading as Austin and Pickersgill Ltd. Their Wear Dockyard had been kept open and delivered its last vessel of the type, *Rondo,* in May 1957 to the Pelton Steam Ship Co. Ltd. of Newcastle, one of the small, colliery-related ship owners mentioned earlier which regularly chartered vessels to the utilities. Four years later, however, it was sold to Stephenson Clarke taking the name *Findon.* Almost a *Chelwood* was the motor vessel *Southwark* of 1958, virtually a sister of the South Metropolitan Gas Company's (by now the South Eastern Gas Board) early post-war *Effra* and *Catford,* and like them intended to serve the East Greenwich gas works.

There were complicated decisions to be made by the collier owning companies: *Chelwood*-sized vessels were still needed but, as noted, the last of these was completed in 1957 and all had been disposed of by the 1980s, replaced by a new generation of North East Coast collier. The success of the *Hudson Deep* experiment coupled with technical developments in the design of single-deck cargo vessels resulted in what was soon to become the Central Electricity Generating Board (CEGB) inviting Stephenson Clarke,

Completed at Burntisland in 1959, Stephenson Clarke's *Storrington* is seen with just one derrick on her mainmast. Other photos show that at times she carried none, and at others shipped four at each mast, presumably when working outside the purely coastal coal trade. Sold in 1968, and renamed *Milos II* and later *Stagan,* she stranded in July 1984 during a delivery voyage to breakers at Karachi. *[Roy Fenton collection]*

William France, Fenwick, Hudson and Cory to negotiate charters and build a series of six large motor colliers of around 7,000 tons deadweight to the single-deck, machinery-aft configuration. All were delivered between 1964 and 1967 with the first, appropriately given the name *Chelwood* by her owner William, France Fenwick when completed in November 1964. As the smaller vessels were phased out of service the CEGB added to the series by chartering similar vessels from other owners, eventually adding some to their own fleet.

But that is another story!

Upper: The oil-fired steam collier *Corstream* was completed in September 1955, her diesel-driven near-sister *Corstar* following a few months later. *Corstream* was sold and renamed *Kyramaruko* in 1972, but stranded off Esbjerg in November of that year. Although refloated, she was fit only for scrap, given her steam machinery and age, and was broken up in Hamburg. *[Roy Fenton collection]*

Middle: The diesel-driven *Southwark* was delivered to the South Eastern Gas Board in February 1958 to practically the same dimensions as *Effra*. As with other relatively modern colliers owned by the nationalised gas industry, the replacement of coal gas by natural gas hastened her sale, and by 1968 she too had gone to Greek owners. Five owners and six names later, the register books lost track of her, deleting her in the 1990s for lack of precise information on her existence. *[Ships in Focus]*

Below: The second *Chelwood* passed to Houlder Brothers as *Oswestry Grange* when France, Fenwick left shipping in 1973. In 1985 she was converted to a barge by Swedish owners, and survived as this under a plethora of owners and names until she stranded on the coast of Somalia in October 2002. *[J. and M. Clarkson]*

JOHN WIGHAM RICHARDSON
Ian Rae

In 1860 John Wigham Richardson, with financial backing from his family, bought a disused shipyard on the north bank of the Tyne, three miles downstream from Newcastle. In 1903 the company's title would be joined with that of another local shipbuilder, creating one of the enduring names in the industrial landscape of Tyneside in the twentieth century.

Born in 1837, John was descended from an old Whitby family. His middle name, Wigham, was his mother's maiden name, and he used Wigham Richardson in business. He was schooled at York by the Society of Friends and, as a quaker, stood by his convictions and never built a warship in his yard. At the age of 16 he joined Senhouse Martindale, a Lloyd's surveyor at Liverpool, to study naval architecture and learn about the shipping industry. Returning home he joined a steam tug builder, Jonathan Robson of Gateshead, as an apprentice draughtsman until 1856. His education continued at University College, London and at the 15th-century university at Tubingen, Baden-Wurttemberg on the Rhine. During his time in Germany he made useful contacts for the years ahead. His university education came to an abrupt end when the collapse of the Northumberland and District Bank put the family finances in disarray. Subsequently, his intention to marry the daughter of a prominent family in Lübeck was overruled by her father. Returning home in 1858 he joined the engineering works of R. and W. Hawthorn at Forth Banks in Newcastle, as a marine engine draughtsman.

However, it was not until March 1860 that the yard was bought by the 23-year old John Wigham Richardson who paid £5,000. The shipyard had three building berths, the largest being 320 feet long, covering four acres. It is difficult to imagine what a primitive place Wallcar was in those days, with no rail connection and no road other than a muddy cart track across fields, along which Wigham Richardson rode on horseback each day from Newcastle. Yet once the business became established the workforce soon reached 200.

In 1859 Wigham Richardson had had the good fortune to meet Charles John Denham Christie and, on taking over the yard, he appointed Christie as its manager, with a promise that if the business succeeded he would become a partner within two years. He was seven years older than Wigham Richardson, and had served his time in a Dumbarton shipyard. At the age of 18 he had gone off to sail around the world and on his return became a manager at the Alexander Denny shipyard in Dumbarton, where he gained experience in liner construction. In 1857 he was on his honeymoon when he received letters informing him that the company had gone bankrupt, and that the Western Bank of Scotland, in which he had invested all his savings, had also stopped payment as a result of a UK-wide banking crash. Christie went to see Isambard Brunel, and was employed in the building and completion of the *Great Eastern*. He suggested to Brunel that the ship would never pay or could even be worked as built, as the 'tween deck height was

The Neptune yard at Walker

In 1842 a John Coutts opened a small shipyard at Wallcar, but it operated for just six years. The name Wallcar was derived from the nearby Hadrian's Wall and the word 'carr' meaning marshy ground. It was a rudimentary settlement, being connected to Newcastle only by one rough road through fields. In due course its name became Walker.

Miller, Ravenhill, Salkeld and Co. of London ran the yard between 1851 and 1855. This company had a yard and engineering works at Blackwall on the Thames, from where they transferred their shipbuilding to the Tyne, launching a total of eight ships which were all towed to the Thames for installation of machinery. Their last ship, the *Tyne*, a 1,603 ton paddle steamer with accommodation for 400 passengers, was launched for the Royal Mail Steam Packet Company's South American routes on 10th August 1854. A week later *Tyne* was towed from the river by two Thames tugs, *Merry Monarch* and *Merry Andrew*. The owners put the yard up for auction in April 1855.

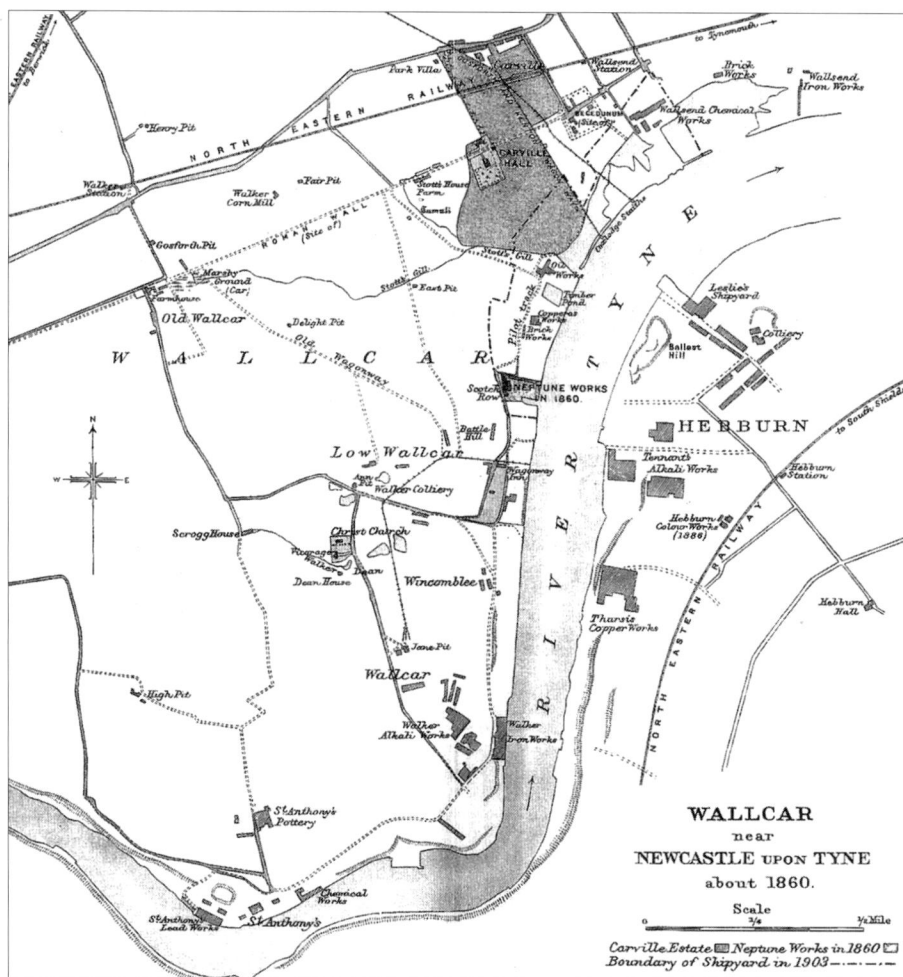

WALLCAR near NEWCASTLE upon TYNE about 1860.

Carville Estate 🔲 Neptune Works in 1860 🔲
Boundary of Shipyard in 1903 —·—·—·—

16 feet. Christie suggested fitting an intermediate deck, but his idea was not adopted.

After taking up his position at Wigham Richardson's Neptune shipyard, Christie achieved renown as a naval architect. For years he personally faired the lines of every ship in the moulding loft, and became acquainted with every detail of the ships' construction. It was fortunate that Wigham Richardson and Christie worked well together as business was slack at the start of their venture, with trade recovering only slowly from a financial crisis in 1857.

The Neptune yard's first ship was the small paddle ferry *Victoria* completed in 1861 for the Isle of Wight to Portsmouth service. No other work came the yard's way until it obtained a 'hull and spars' order for the 958-ton sailing ship *Ambrose*. The £9,900 contract was with a ships' chandler and speculator from Sunderland. However, the contract turned sour, resulting in a two-year lawsuit, but with victory for the shipbuilder who was awarded costs of £1,800.

Wigham Richardson was a very affable man, and was fluent in German, French and Latin. His penchant for Latin verses saw these being inscribed in stone in appropriate places around the shipyard. He was also responsible for a large ornate wooden sundial on the gable end of the building which housed the shipyard's time office and its main gatehouse. The inscription below the sundial noted that Wallcar time was six minutes behind Greenwich and added that 'Watching these fleeting hours soon past, remember that which comes at last'. The sundial and a photograph of the original gable end are now at the Discovery Museum at Newcastle.

The first ship to be built by John Wigham Richardson in 1860 was *Victoria*, a 65 foot paddle steamer for the Ryde Ferry Company. Priced at just £698 she was sub-contracted from Andrew Leslie and Co. who supplied the engine. She can claim to be the Isle of Wight's first ro-ro as her square stern bulwark served as a watertight door that could be hinged down to allow carts or cattle to be driven on board.

Yard number 2, the iron barque *Ambrose,* was a 'hull and spars' contract ordered by John Smurthwaite of Sunderland, but sold before completion to Liverpool owners for the trade to India. In 1882 she was renamed *Willowbank*, and three years later sold to Andrew Weir of Glasgow. She was his first ship and gave rise to his famous 'bank' nomenclature. In December 1895 she was run down and sunk in thick weather off Portland by the Red Star liner *City of Berlin* (5,562/1895).

Sir Herbert Maddock was a river paddle steamer built for the Indus Flotilla Company and launched on 29th October 1864 by the shipbuilder's sister. Named after the owner's Vice Chairman and a former Governor of Bengal she was designed to tow barges into the Punjab, taking in imports such as railway lines and British troops to their garrisons. On return voyages she carried cotton for export to the Lancashire mills. After trials on the Tyne the ship was dismantled and shipped out to the owner's building yard at Kurrachee, and relaunched on 12th October 1866.

155

Contacts and contracts

During his early shipbuilding career Wigham Richardson travelled extensively, expanding and cementing business relationships with ship owners. For example, in 1863 he met Captain Durham, the British representative of the Armenian trading house Apcar of Calcutta, who were opium and tea traders. During April 1864 he married Marian Thoel, the daughter of a Hamburg businessman, and they were to have three sons and two daughters. The connection with Hamburg proved useful as the yard was to build many ships for German owners, beginning in 1865 with the *Ruhr*, a ferry for carrying coal trucks across the River Rhine.

As a quaker Wigham Richardson was deeply concerned about the welfare of his employees, and founded a workers' benevolent trust, offering some of the benefits of a trade union. As his workforce grew it became apparent that housing would have to be provided to retain his employees. So in 1873 the nearby 70-acre Carville Estate was acquired for £30,000. The seventeenth century hall was built mainly from stone taken from the Roman wall, a common occurrence with many houses, farms and castles in Northumberland.

In 1872 the company decided to begin constructing engines and boilers, with an engine shop being added at the northern end of the shipyard. Originally this was intended to service just the yard's output, but it expanded to supply other shipyards. The management of this shop was placed in the hands of John Tweedy, who became a partner in 1879. In 1890 he patented a version of the quadruple expansion engine which was installed in a number of ships built by the Neptune yard.

John Wigham Richardson had many interests, and in shipbuilding and engineering these ranged from the construction of Greek triremes to the details of compound engines. In 1874 he published a pamphlet criticising the rules of Lloyd's Register, which he claimed encouraged the building of unduly weak ships. Responding to this and other criticisms, the classification society eventually changed its rules. In 1890 Wigham Richardson was elected President of the North East Coast Institution of Engineers and Shipbuilders

With the cyclical nature of shipping and shipbuilding, business proved difficult for periods during the 1870s and 1880s. For instance, in 1883 the company delivered ten ships with a total gross tonnage of 20,493, but in 1886 the total had fallen to just five of 4,560 gross tons, and only five other orders were booked in the entire year. In response, an aggressive sales drive was begun in Europe utilising existing contacts. The result was that, up to the amalgamation with C.S. Swan and Co. in 1903, the Neptune yard was the most successful on Tyneside in securing merchant ship orders from overseas, with over two thirds of its tonnage destined for foreign customers.

The contract for the Spanish *Alfonso XII* in 1888, although completed at a loss, was seen by many owners as demonstrating the capabilities of the yard. The passenger ship was the largest merchant vessel yet launched on the river. As the yard's portfolio of designs grew, it concentrated on dry cargo ships and emigrant carriers such as the Italian *Rosario*.

From 1893 they built 15 Irish Sea vessels to carry passengers and cattle for owners in Cork. The growing market for oil tankers was neglected, however, and it was not until 1912, well after the amalgamation with their next door neighbour, that the Neptune yard built its first tanker, *San Dunstano*, part of a 19-ship order placed by Eagle Oil, 17 of which built on the Tyne

A fine view of the Neptune shipyard in early 1888, with work on *Alfonso XII* well advanced. The only piece of mechanical handling equipment evident is the rail-mounted steam crane, seen exhausting steam in the centre of the photograph. The horse is possibly going to move the crane and the accompanying truck along the tightly-curved track. Note the spars for the scaffolding lying in the foreground, the iron work to the right and the ramp up which fittings would have been dragged.

What is considered Charles Christie's masterpiece, the 5,063 gross ton passenger and mail steamer *Alfonso XII* was launched on 20th March 1888 for Compania Trasatlantica of Barcelona. Originally ordered as a cargo ship in April 1886, the design was subsequently amended and she was re-ordered in January 1888 to become the largest merchant ship yet built on the Tyne. With accommodation for 289 passengers and 800 troops she was designed to service Spain's colonies, the owners receiving a subsidy from the Spanish government.

Alfonso XII had 2,000 cubic feet of refrigerated spaces, artificial ventilation to the lower 'tween decks, hydraulic cargo handling and steering gear and electric light throughout. The ship was launched by the twin daughters of the ship's master Jose San Paedro, each breaking a bottle of champagne on one side of the bow. Such was the interest created in the ship on completion in September 1888 that she was moored in the river and opened to the general public with the proceeds of tickets sales donated to convalescent homes at Whitley Bay.

Christie's design was inspired by the experience he had gained when working on similar contracts at Denny's yard on the Clyde. Despite the kudos the ship earned for Christie and the shipyard, the company made a £15,080 loss on the contract.

Despite Wigham Richardson's aversion to building warships, on delivery to Spain six five-ton guns were installed on the upper deck. She began her maiden voyage from Barcelona to Vera Cruz on 25th October 1888, and subsequently called regularly at Cuba.

In 1898 tensions between the USA and Spain boiled over after the sinking of the battleship USS *Maine* in Havana harbour with the loss of 260 officers and men. War was declared on 21st April 1898. On 5th July *Alfonso XII* attempted to break the naval blockade that the USA had in force around Cuba. She was chased by several warships including USS *Hawk*, a 545-ton armed yacht, but with her speed of 15 knots she was able to outrun her pursuers. That night she attempted to enter the harbour at Port Mariel, but ran on to a reef in the darkness. In the morning reinforcements in the form of USS *Castine* destroyed the stranded *Alfonso XII* with gunfire.

Rosario (1,900/1887) was one of 13 emigrant ships built for Italian owners. Around 2,000 gross tons and just 280 feet long, each managed to cram in over a thousand passengers G.B. Lavarello's *Rosario* was built to run to South America. Sold in 1898 to Compagnie de Navigation Mixte of Marseilles, and renamed *Djurjura* she ran on North African services. During the First World War she was used as a troopship but sank at Malta on 14th December 1915 after a collision.

In 1899 J. Wigham Richardson and Co. became a limited liability company, with its founder appointed managing director. On the amalgamation with C.S. Swan Hunter Ltd. on 15th September 1903 he became a director of the joint concern and remained so until his death in 1905. By the time of the amalgamation the yard had produced 135 ships, totalling 213,373 grt for the home market and 166 ships of 323,344 grt for overseas, the later comprising 60 per cent of its output. The engine works had completed 185 engines, boilers and auxiliaries for themselves and for a total of 76 other shipbuilders. The following pages illustrate some of Wigham Richardson's output.

Sons and daughters
Son of the founder, Phillip Wigham Richardson followed his father into the business, but after five years of management training he left and changed course, moving to London in 1892 and turning to ship management, agency and financial work. In 1900 he also became a Lloyd's underwriter. In 1892 he became manager of the Trident Line, running betwen Marseilles to Odessa. By 1894 he was operating a dozen ships under the auspices of London Steamers Ltd., the Manchester and District Shipping Co., and the Wingrove Steamship Co. Ltd. Several other single ship companies were also managed,

although he maintained his partnership in the shipbuilding company, his business contacts especially in France helping to win orders for the shipyard at Low Walker. After the loss of two ships during the First World War, he moved away from ship owning into finance, although his company is listed as manager of a number of Greek-owned steamers.

Phillip was a keen sportsman and competed in rifle competitions in the Olympics in both 1908 and 1912. In 1922 he was elected to Parliament, serving until 1931, and became the first Baron Weybridge in 1929.

John Denham Christie also followed in his father's footsteps, and served his apprenticeship as a draughtsman with John Elder and Co. at Govan, and later with other local north east coast builders, a common practice for sons of yard owners. Returning to Low Walker he became actively involved with the design of passenger and mail ships and of cable ships, the latter becoming something of a company specialty. His two children followed him into the company, his daughter Susan Mary becoming the first female naval architect in the U.K.

Both sons would become chairman of Swan Hunter and Wigham Richardson Ltd., John Denham Christie between 1930 and 1939, and Phillip Wigham Richardson from 1945 to 1953.

Above: *Van Swoll* (1,624/1897) was the larger of two ships built to operate in the Dutch East Indies and given a draft of 17.5 feet which allowed them to serve shallow creeks. In 1928 she was sold to Singapore owners and renamed *Edendale*. Operating in far eastern waters for all her career, she survived until January 1955 when she was bombed by Chinese Nationalist aircraft at Swatow, having brought 200 tons of general cargo from Hong Kong. The ship turned on to her side. The owners sent another ship to pick up the crew, but they could not be found. The

Chinese authorities refused to give any information, but eventually it transpired that the crew had made their escape overland.

Opposite page top: *Potosi* (5,970/1900) was one of two steamers ordered from Wigham Richardson's yard in February 1899 by the Pacific Steam Navigation Co. Ltd.

At the time of her launch a delegation from the Russian Volunteer Fleet were in the North East looking to

acquire ships. Suffering a decline in trade, Pacific Steam decided to sell the ship, accepting an offer of £109,000. She was hurriedly converted into a transport for 2,000 troops and renamed *Kazan*, sailing from the Tyne for Odessa on 15th September 1899.

During her early career she was used to transport forced labourers and prisoners to Siberia to complete the Siberian railway. When the Russo-Japanese War broke out in 1904 she was at Vladivostok, redesignated as a coal carrier for the cruiser squadron. Later that year she was damaged by

Russian shelling and later sank at Port Arthur. Salvaged by the Japanese Navy she was renamed *Kasato Maru*.

This phase of her career saw *Kasato Maru* carrying Japanese emigrants to South America, serving as a hospital ship for the Japanese Navy during the invasion of China in 1927, and then relegated to carrying only cargo

In 1930 she was converted into a floating crab cannery to work in the Sea of Okhotsk. On 9th August 1945 she was lying off the coast of Kamchatka along with another ship providing storage facilities for fish. The U.S.S.R. now belatedly declared war on Japan and, as the *Kasato Maru* prepared to leave, Soviet bombers raided the facility and sank the old ship.

Argenfels (5,654/1901) (right) was one of some 20 ships built by the yard before the merger for DDG 'Hansa' of Bremen. She was seized by French authorities at Saigon on the outbreak of the First World War, although apparently never renamed for French service. In 1921 still as *Argenfels* she was sold to Greek owners to become *Dimitrios M. Diacakis*, and was broken up at Genoa in 1932.

In 1902 Wigham Richardson received an order from the Telegraph Construction and Maintenance Co. Ltd. of London for the world's largest cable laying ship, the 7,976 grt *Colonia*. The shipyard's design department developed such an understanding of the requirements for this type of ship that they served a niche in the market and over the next 82 years the yard built a further 23 cable layers.

Colonia was built to lay a cable from Vancouver to New Zealand and Australia and in her 26 years of service laid 80,700 miles of cable worldwide. In 1928 she was sold to A/S Thor Dahl of Sandefjord, and converted to the whale factory ship *Torodd*. She was sold on to another Norwegian owner before coming under the German flag as the *Sudmeer* in 1937, spending two more whaling seasons in the Antarctic. Whilst being used as a transport for whale oil and armaments, she was torpedoed and sunk by Russian aircraft off Honningsvaag on 14th October 1944.

Choy Sang (2,284/1902) and her sister *Kwong Sang* (2,283/1902) were built for the Indo China Steam Navigation Co. Ltd., and both were to succumb to typhoons. *Choy Sang* was wrecked 14 miles north of Swatow on 2nd August 1922. *Kwong Sang* left Shanghai on 8th August 1931 for Swatow, but was driven ashore on the island of Fuyan the next day. Three survivors from a crew of 50 fell into the hands of pirates. Four steamships were sent to search plus a destroyer and a Chinese gunboat. A military force was landed between Funing and Santuao Bays, and compelled the pirates to release the men.

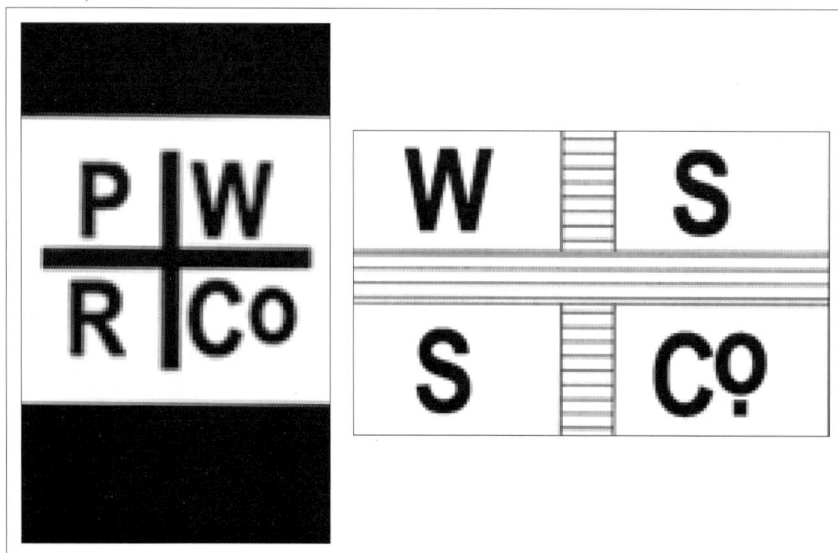

Funnel and flag used by ships managed by Phillip Wigham Richardson. The cross on the funnel is blue, the letters red. The houseflag illustrated is that of the managed Wingrove Steamship Co. Ltd., and again the letters are red and the cross blue. A plain black funnel is reported for this company. *[J.L. Loughran]*

This frieze was placed above the main staircase leading to the directors offices in the Neptune Yard. *[All illustrations are from the Author's collection]*

SOURCES AND ACKNOWLEDGEMENTS

We thank all who gave permission for their photographs to be used, and for help in finding photographs we are particularly grateful to Tony Smith, Jim McFaul and David Whiteside of the World Ship Photo Library; to Ian Farquhar, F.W. Hawks, Peter Newall, Russell Priest, William Schell; and to David Hodge and Bob Todd of the National Maritime Museum.

Research sources have included the Registers of William Schell and Tony Starke, 'Lloyd's Register', 'Lloyd's Confidential Index', 'Lloyd's Shipping Index', 'Lloyd's War Losses', 'Mercantile Navy Lists', 'Marine News', 'Sea Breezes' and 'Shipbuilding and Shipping Record'. Use of the facilities of the World Ship Society, particularly Alan Watt at its Chatham archive, the Guildhall Library, the National Archives are acknowledged.

Chelwood to Chelwood
Sources include published histories of William France, Fenwick; Stephenson Clarke; William Cory and Christian Salvesen; 'The Steam Colliers' by Captain J.A. MacRae and C.V. Waine, 'Gas and Electricicity Colliers' by Roy Fenton and 'The Empire Ships' by Sawyer and Mitchell. Articles published by Roy Fenton in 'Record' issues 17, 18, 20 and 49; Captain A.W. Kinghorn (21); Graham Atkinson (31); John Lingwood (50, 53, 54) were also consulted. Information on the Second World War convoys were obtained from 'The Allied Convoy System 1939-1945' compiled by Arnold Hague. Reference to the Patrick Stephens publication 'British Vessels Lost at Sea 1939-1945' is also noted.

Fowey's powered coasters
Ward-Jackson's 'Ships and Shipbuilders of a West Country Port' proved a very useful starting point. The ships' histories were researched using the usual sources and customs registers at the National Archives, Kew. Bill Schell helped nail the story of *A.B. Sherman* using 'Lloyd's War Losses: The First World War' and Spindler's work on U-boat successes.

Aberdeen's scratcher trawler fleet
Sources include lists of Aberdeen-built trawlers and their histories compiled by the late Wilfred M. Dodds; newspaper cuttings from the 'Press and Journal' and 'Evening Express' held at the library of Aberdeen Journals Ltd.; the shipping registers for the port of Aberdeen held by Aberdeen City Archives; archive copies of 'Fishing News' held at Aberdeen Central Library; 'Sputniks and Spinningdales, a history of pocket trawlers' by Sam Henderson and Peter Drummond (The History Press, 2011).

PUTTING THE RECORD STRAIGHT

Letters, additions, amendments and photographs relating to features in any issues of 'Record' are welcomed (one of the letters below harks back to issue 41). Letters may be lightly edited. Note that comments on multi-part articles are consolidated and included in the issue of 'Record' following the final part. Senders of e-mails are asked to provide their postal address.

Scheldt shipping sequel
The *Bertha* that was the first ship to reach Antwerp in November 1944 ('Record' 58 page 66) was probably the 487grt salvage vessel built in 1905 for the London and South Western Railway. She was converted in 1933 by Metal Industries Ltd. for salvaging the German warships scuttled at Scapa Flow. Taken over by the Admiralty in 1940, she became *Topmast No. 6* in 1947, scrapped at Antwerp the following year.

Splendid series of photos.
IAN BUXTON, 12 Grand Parade, Tynemouth, North Shields, Tyne and Wear NE30 4JS
By a remarkable coincidence, Bertha *is featured in the article on Southern Railway cargo steamers in this issue. Ed.*

I will take issue with two items regarding Great Lakes shipping in 'Record' 58.

First off the photo of the *Lachinedoc* in the lovely spread of photos from the Scheldt. The caption states she had seven holds - no way! It was seven hatches, but two cargo holds. I am looking at the 1930 American Bureau of Shipping Great Lakes Register book as I write. The big 600-foot full 'lakers' typically had three cargo holds, even though they might have up to 24 hatches (on 12-foot centres).

Then we come to page 80 where the charter of the two 'Jeeps' to Hall Corporation of Canada is mentioned for the 'coal trade'. While the origins of the firm lay in the coal business in the 19th century, in the post-Second World War period, up to the opening of the St. Lawrence Seaway in 1959, the firm's primary business lay in carrying pulpwood from the Gulf of St. Lawrence to supply paper mills in upstate New York. Grain would have been the primary 'backhaul' from transit elevators in the range between Port Colborne and Prescott, Ontario to the export elevators in Montreal, Sorel and Quebec. There would have been some coal traffic from American Lake Erie and Lake Ontario ports for Gulf of St. Lawrence destinations, but that would have been much more likely to have gone in the 'canallers' rather than the 'Jeeps'.
BILL SCHELL, 334 South Franklin Street, Holbrook, MA 02343, USA

Stuart Prince at war
Looking back at some old 'Records' I came across the Prince Line articles. In issue 41 page 10 you ask for details of the Second World War career of *Stuart Prince*. She was a 'Landing Ship Fighter Direction', one of ten such ships used for the detection of enemy air activity and the control of our own over areas of invasion beaches. They were fitted with all the best radar and communications equipment and were placed in harms way so as not to risk capital ships with similar equipment

in this role. *Stuart Prince* was armed with 24 20mm AA guns for this role. She was returned to her owners in 1945.

Information comes from 'Warships of World War 2, Part Eight, Landing Craft' by H.T. Lenton and J.J. Colledge; published Ian Allan, London, 1963. Their sources will be impeccable.
TERRY BOLTON, 46 High Street, Berkhamsted, Hertfordshire HP4 2BP

On Messageries Maritimes
I thoroughly enjoyed Dr. Burel's good humoured appraisal of Messageries Maritimes. Having spent half my career in government ships I wholeheartedly concur that government should not be involved in ship design! Given the short derricks, unreliable winches and inherent stability problems the crew probably deserved the fine French dining arrangements. I frequently saw Messageries Maritimes' ships in the Far East and Australian waters in the early 1960s and thought them fine looking ships - exemplified in the back-cover photo of the *Var*. One odd feature I always thought was how high the lifeboats were carried - who else had lifeboats above the bridge? I have frequently employed seven-ton survey launches - launch and recovery in anything over force 5 was a decidedly ticklish operation and they were only 25 feet above the sea in their chocks. Those MM lifeboats hanging from sky-hooks 50 feet above the water would be horrible to manage in much of a sea I imagine.

John Goble raises an interesting point regarding the *Rosaleen*, page 58, issue 57. In that the topping lift is much lighter than the purchase mentioned I can only conclude that, lacking steam power with the ship aground, the crew has resorted to old fashioned Armstrong's Patent to shift something.
JOHN ANDERSON, 523 Louise Road, Ladysmith, British Columbia V9G 1W7, Canada

Irish Bay snippet
Further to Ian Wilson's article about Irish Bay Lines, *Dingle Bay*, ex Reardon Smith's *New Westminster City* was built by William Gray's Wear yard. She was bombed and severely damaged at Murmansk on 3rd April 1942 following arrival from the Mersey. Abandoned as a constructive total loss, she was anchored in shallow water until salvaged jointly by the Royal Navy and the Soviets. In March 1947 she was towed to Penarth and transferred to the Ministry of Transport. In 1948 she was sold to Irish Bay Lines and in November sent to Trieste for reconditioning, including the rebuilding of her accommodation block and funnel.
A.D.FROST, 32 Oakfield Close, Sunderland SR3 3RT.

Corrections and additions
Several readers have ticked off the editors for describing *Jadotville* on page 120 of 'Record' 58 as a sister of *Baudouinville*. We should have said fleet mate.

David Whiteside notes that the photograph of *Selbo* on page 118 would have been taken on or about 24th November 1938, when she made her only visit to Preston, bringing pulp from Norway.

FOWEY'S POWERED COASTERS
Roy Fenton

The 'South West Scenes' visit to Fowey in 'Record' 57 stimulated research into the port's two fleets which included powered vessels. After initial success, both had self-inflicted problems which drove them out of business.

Toyne, Carter and Co.
Not only did they manage the only fleet of steam ships ever registered at Fowey, but Charles Louis Toyne and his partner John Peers Carter were most unusual in that they sold their steam fleet and went into sail, although with disastrous consequences.

Charles Toyne was born about 1870, probably in Fowey. John Carter came from Connah's Quay where Captain Henry Carter – undoubtedly his father – had been a junior partner of the well-known Coppack family between 1883 and 1898. Several of Coppack's vessels were owned, for a time, in the name of Coppack, Carter and Co. Charles Toyne and John Carter are believed to have gone into business as ship brokers in 1896, although Toyne already had minor shareholdings in locally-owned vessels, sufficient to offer himself as ship's husband, and run the ships' shoreside affairs from his office.

Beginning in 1897, the partners' steam ship owning followed a clear trajectory, with a ship being added almost yearly for six years. What was impressive is how the quality of their ships rose, with the first being 41-years-old, the second 16 and the third 22, and then three successive steamers delivered new by highly reputable builders of steam coasters. Finance came from floating five single-ship companies, logically if prosaically named, with the *Foy* being ordered early in 1901 to replace the unfortunate *Norma* in the books of the Fowey (No. 3) Steamship Co. Ltd. This replacement was a somewhat unusual practice for a single-ship company; the companies' articles of association typically providing that, when its sole ship was sold or lost, the company would be automatically wound up. The foundering of *Norma* in January 1901 was the only loss the little fleet of steamers suffered, even in the face of hostilities which three of its ships faced during the whole or part of the First World War, although the company was deprived of the use of *Torfrey* which was unfortunate enough to be in Hamburg in August 1914.

Official returns and other documents survive from four of the six single ship companies (see below). In each case the authorised share capital would closely reflect the cost of purchasing the company's ship. For instance, the capital was £9,000 for the Par Steamship Co. Ltd. whose contract with Fullertons for the *Par* was for £8,500. Only for this company was the number of shares bought (in other words, the paid-up capital) sufficient to pay for the steamer outright, and in other cases the balance had to be made up with a mortgage on the ship. For instance, floating the Fowey (No. 4) Steamship Co. Ltd. raised £6,890 out of its target of £10,500, the latter figure reflecting the price of *Torfrey* which the company ordered. To raise the full amount the steamer had to be mortgaged for £3,500 to a member of the Holman family of Camborne.

The partners' shareholdings in the companies they managed were relatively modest, for example at the winding up of the Fowey (No.3) Steamship Co. Ltd. in 1918, Carter had 38 of the 671 paid up shares, and Toyne 39, with a few held by their wives. These holdings contrasts with the 54 held by John M. Bennetts, a Cornish coal merchant and a coaster owner in his own right, and who was an initial subscriber to at least three other Toyne, Carter companies. Other subscribers and shareholders were divided between Cornwall and London, the Cornishmen being mainly local businessmen.

Carrying china clay coastwise would have been a natural cargo for the Toyne, Carter managed fleet, especially as – being shipbrokers – the partners would have no difficulty finding cargoes in Fowey. Incoming cargoes would often be coal for Cornish ports, including Penzance where shareholder John Bennetts was trading. Determining trading patterns for steam coasters, whose voyages would usually last less than a week, is notoriously difficult unless cargo books have survived. There is evidence from photographs that *Par* visited the Manchester Ship Canal, and the ships were very familiar in Preston during Toyne, Carter's management (see table), although surprisingly the Preston photographers seem not to have captured their images. The accompanying photographs show that *Foy*, *Torfrey* and *Deerhound* were docked, for survey and repair, in the Richmond Dry Dock at Appledore.

The dissolution of the steam fleet seems to have been as carefully

Toyne, Carter single-ship companies			
Name	Ships	Dates	Paid up/ authorised capital
Fowey Steamship Co. Ltd.	Stockton	1897–~1906	?
Fowey (No. 2) Steamship Co. Ltd.	Deerhound	1898–~1916	?
Fowey (No. 3) Steamship Co. Ltd.	Norma, Foy	1899–1918	£6,710/£7,000
Fowey (No. 4) Steamship Co. Ltd.	Torfrey	1900–1919	£6,890/£10,500
Par (No. 1) Steamship Co. Ltd.	Par	1901–1919	£9,000/9,000
Stockton Steamship Co. Ltd.	Stockton	1906–1910	£920/£1,100

Visits to Preston by Toyne, Carter steamers		
Stockton	1897-1907	31 calls, all with clay, occasionally returning to the south west with coal.
Deerhound	1898-1917	62 calls, all with clay occasionally returning to the South West with coal.
Norma	1899-1902	5 calls, all with clay.
Torfrey	1900-1919	64 calls with clay, 2 in 1903 with Jersey potatoes, 1 in 1908 from Hamburg with sugar (possibly on charter to William Robertson), 2 visits arrived light (in ballast), took coal out.
Par	1902-1919	35 calls with clay, usually loading coal out
Foy	1902-1919	100 calls with clay, usually loading coal out. 5 final calls with coal, usually from Cardiff.

managed as its acquisition. Just after her fiftieth birthday, in 1907 *Stockton* found a new owner in Hull. *Deerhound* lasted until 1916 when her 34-year-old iron hull – probably worth little more than her scrap value a few years earlier – readily found a buyer thanks to wartime inflation of demand and ship prices. The astronomical prices which coasters could command in 1918 and 1919 undoubtedly persuaded the partners to liquidate the companies owning *Par*, *Torfrey* and *Foy* and sell off these ships. Perhaps the most spectacular gain resulted from the detention of the *Torfrey* at Hamburg in August 1914. In June 1925 the surviving shareholders accepted £40,000 from the German government under the terms of the Treaty of Versailles. This would reflect loss of earnings and damage, but even so was very generous. The steamer was valued at just £8,840 in 1916, and on disposal in May 1919 would undoubtedly have made a very substantial profit, notwithstanding repairs which would have been needed after serving the German Army.

Two of the Toyne, Carter steam fleet in the Richmond Dry Dock at Appledore. *Deerhound* (above), date unknown and *Torfrey* (below) in late summer 1908. *[Both North Devon Maritime Trust Collection]*

Disastrously into sail

The cautious approach to management of the steam fleet discussed above contrasts strongly with the chaos of the partnership's later venture into sail. This began in 1917 with the acquisition of the *Earl Cairns*, a 34-year-old schooner that had been built on Deeside, and was currently owned there.

Earl Cairns was a conventional choice, but this can hardly be said of the *A.B. Sherman*, one of the very few U.S.-built sailing coasters to come on to the British register during the twentieth century. Built in 1883 in Boston, she had been intended for the U.S. East Coast coal trade, and ran mainly out of Virginia, her final U.S. owner being based in Philadelphia. The circumstances of her sale were also highly unusual. The high freight rates obtainable in 1917 led her owners to send her to Le Havre with a cargo, but on 26th June 1917 *A.B. Sherman* was attacked by a U-boat off the Scillies. Some accounts have her attempting to supply the U-boat and being taken as a prize, but in fact the submarine tried to sink her with a scuttling charge. She was towed into St. Marys badly damaged, and later taken to Plymouth. This was shortly before the United States entered the First World War.

A.B. Sherman was stripped down in Devonport Dockyard, but in September 1919 was sold to Toyne, Carter and Co. Ltd. who had her towed to Fowey. They gave the work of putting her back into service to the Slade family's shipyard at Polruan, once Fowey's most successful builder of wooden sailing ships. But *A.B. Sherman* proved too big for the Slade yard (at 168 feet in length she was the second largest vessel ever owned in Fowey), and the work was carried out at Pont Pill, where a surplus army hut was erected to facilitate the repair work. This work was extensive, as during the scuttling attempt she had a bomb placed against her foremast, and was holed by shells on both sides above the waterline. Toyne, Carter insisted that the repair work was carried out to a high enough standard to satisfy the surveyors of Lloyd's Register, and this extended both the duration of repairs and their cost. Amongst a number of expensive modifications, she was re-rigged from three to four masts, her running bowsprit was removed, a false keel was fitted and she had many hull planks renewed. The work was not completed until October 1921, by when it had cost £6,535 on top of her initial purchase price of £16,627. But by then the demand for ships, vastly inflated by war losses and accompanying disruption, had given way to a glut, and a vessel which had cost Toyne, Carter over £23,000 was independently valued at just £1,100.

This was by no means the end of the company's losses on *A.B. Sherman*, as she was quite unable to meet her voyage costs. In his book 'Ships and Shipbuilders of a West Country Port', Ward-Jackson reports that, in only a few months of trading, she lost Toyne, Carter a further £25,000. This figure seems hard to believe, and probably includes the cost or acquiring and refitting the vessel. In the spring of 1922 *A.B. Sherman* arrived at Livorno with a cargo of china clay, leaking badly despite the work which Lloyd's Register's surveyors had insisted be done. During 1923 she was sold to a Italian owner reportedly for just £500.

The British-built schooner *Mary Peers* appears under Toyne, Carter's name in 'Lloyd's Register' for 1921. She had been built in Newquay in 1875 for a Chester River owner, her ownership involving Henry Charles Carter from about 1885. It is likely that his share passed to John Carter of Fowey in 1896, and that in 1921 Toyne, Carter and Co. became its largest shareholder, with 38 of the 64 shares, with John Carter retaining 16 shares and the rest still owned on Deeside. This was the year in which Charles Toyne died, presumably leaving Carter in control of the business. *Mary Peers* and *Earl Cairns* would trade mainly with china clay. But as if to emphasise that the age of the sailing ship really was over, *Mary Peers* was lost in Whitsand Bay in December 1923, although fortunately her crew was rescued. With Toyne gone, and probably much of the partnership's accumulated capital lost as well, it is not surprising that *Earl Cairns* was sold in 1924, ending the 27-year-career of Toyne, Carter as ship owners. It is ironic that the partners started in steam and apparently did well, only to lose out when attempting to run sailing vessels.

Fleet list: Toyne, Carter and Co.

1. STOCKTON 1897-1907 Iron
O.N. 16223 407g 226n.
158.3 x 25.8 x 13.4 feet.
2-cyl. by George Stephenson and Co., Newcastle-upon-Tyne.
1873: C. 2-cyl. by Blair and Co. Ltd., Stockton-on-Tees; 80 NHP.
1856: Launched by M. Pearse and Co., Stockton-on-Tees (Yard No. 10).
18.2.1857: Registered in the ownership of the Stockton and London Screw Steam Ship Company, Stockton-on-Tees as STOCKTON.
2.11.1869: Owners became the Stockton and London Steam Shipping Company, Stockton-on-Tees.
18.10.1870: Owners became the Stockton and London Steam Shipping Co. Ltd., Stockton-on-Tees.
1881: Owners became the Tees Union Shipping Company, Middlesbrough.
1881: Sold to George Bazeley and Sons, Penzance.
24.1.1882: Registered in Penzance.

30.9.1891: Owners became George P., William J. and Sidney G. Bazeley, Penzance.
19.3.1897: Acquired by the Fowey Steamship Co. Ltd. (Charles L. Toyne, manager), Fowey.
28.7.1906: Owners became the Stockton Steamship Co. Ltd. (Toyne, Carter and Co., managers), Fowey.
6.6.1907: Sold to Robert Carson, trading as T. Walker and Co. (Vicars H. Walker, manager), Hull.
15.12.1909: Foundered off Anderby near Skegness, Lincolnshire whilst on a voyage from Goole to Shoreham with a cargo of coal.
24.3.1910: Register closed.

2. DEERHOUND 1898-1916 Iron
O.N. 87030 443g 271n.
159.6 x 24.0 x 12.2 feet.
C. 2-cyl. by R.H. Pearson and Co., Glasgow; 70 NHP.
10.1882: Launched by Forrest and Son, Millwall, London (Yard No. 1156) for George H. Walker and Thomas H.

Above: *Stockton* of 1857 photographed at Goole. *[J. and M. Clarkson collection]*
Below: *Deerhound* in the River Avon, probably early in her long career. *[E.N. Taylor]*

Howard, London as DEERHOUND.
14.3.1898: Sold to Lacey Brown, London (Charles L. Toyne, Fowey, manager).
18.3.1898: Acquired by the Fowey (No.2) Steamship Co. Ltd. (Charles L. Toyne, manager), Fowey.
1.6.1916: Sold to the Ferrum Steamship Co. Ltd. (G.T. Gillie and Co., managers), Newcastle-upon-Tyne.
13.5.1919: Sold to Wettern Brothers Ltd., London.
9.7.1925: Register closed on sale to Louis Hermans, Antwerp, Belgium.
23.9.1930: Grounded on Whitton Sands, River Humber and, swinging to one side, was in collision with the steamer LAKEWOOD (570/1919) which was following her, after which she sank. She was on a voyage from Goole to Bruges with a cargo of coal. Her crew of 15 got away in boats.

3. NORMA 1899-1902 Iron
O.N. 67822 507g 157n.
174.4 x 26.5 x 12.2 feet.
C. 2-cyl. by Kincaid, Donald and Co., Greenock; 86 NHP.
5.1877: Launched by J.E. Scott and Co., Greenock (Yard No. 17).
30.6.1877: Registered in the ownership of the Humber Steamship Co. Ltd., Goole as NORMA.
4.4.1895: Transferred to the Goole Steam Shipping Co. Ltd., Goole.
21.11.1895: Sold to Owen L. Harries, Thomas Harries and Hugh E. Harries, trading as Harries Brothers and Co., Swansea.
8.4.1899: Acquired by the Fowey (No.3) Steamship Co. Ltd. (Toyne, Carter and Co., managers), Fowey.
28.1.1902: Foundered six miles south east of the Longships whilst on a voyage from Newport to Fowey with a cargo of coal.
According to other accounts, including that in her Fowey register, she was abandoned off Trevose Head 28.1.1902, after which the Spanish steamer ELANTSOBE (2,398/1899) took her in tow, but she sank off Land's End on 4.2.1902.

4. TORFREY 1900-1919
O.N. 95378 429g 167n.
167.9 x 25.1 x 9.5 feet.
C. 2-cyl. by Ross and Duncan, Govan; 88 NHP, 700 IHP, 10.25 knots.
10.1900: Completed by John Fullerton and Co., Paisley (Yard No. 156).
22.10.1900: Registered in the ownership of the Fowey (No.4)

Steamship Co. Ltd. (Toyne, Carter and Co., managers), Fowey as TORFREY.
8.1914: Detained at Hamburg.
6.1916: German Army transport
12.1918: Returned to owners.
26.5.1919: Sold to Onesimus Dorey, Guernsey.
26.2.1929: Sold to Gracechurch Transports Ltd. (Richards, Longstaff and Co. Ltd., managers), London.
12.3.1929: Renamed YORKRIVER.
1.7.1932: Sold to James C. Screech, Appledore.
1.10.1932: Sold to Samuel Gray, Belfast.
30.12.1933: Sold to Alfred H. Smith, Shenfield, Essex.
25.1.1934: Sold to Michele Cacace, Genoa, Italy and renamed REGINA CACACE.
1935: Broken up during second quarter.

5. PAR 1902-1919
O.N. 95739 436g 141n.
155.0 x 27.0 x 10.6 feet.
C. 2-cyl. by Ross and Duncan, Govan; 88 NHP, 650 IHP, 10.5 knots.
3.1902: Completed by John Fullerton and Co., Paisley (Yard No. 163).
1.4.1902: Registered in the ownership of the Par (No.1) Steamship Co. Ltd. (Toyne, Carter and Co., managers), Fowey as PAR.
9.1.1919: Sold to Town Line (London) Ltd. (Harrison, Sons and Co., managers), London.
15.2.1919: Renamed OAKTOWN.
13.3.1923: Sold to William J. Duncan trading as Aberdeen Steam Coasters, Aberdeen.
8.4.1926: Sold by William M. Barkley and Sons Ltd. (John Kelly Ltd.), Belfast.

Torfrey. [David Whiteside collection]

Par as *Oaktown*, arriving Preston when owned between 1926 and 1933 by William Barkley and Sons Ltd., a subsidiary of John Kelly Ltd., Belfast. *[J. and M. Clarkson]*

15.11.1933: Sold to Alfred H. Smith, Shenfield, Essex.

30.5.1934: Register closed on sale to A. Fleurbaey, Antwerp, Belgium and renamed STE. MARIE.

1935: Sold to M.A. Karageorgis, Piraeus, Greece and renamed MARINOS.

1935: Sold to Petros M. Nomikos Ltd. and Société Hellenique de Produits Chimiqueset Engrais (Petros M. Nomikos Ltd., managers), Piraeus, Greece and renamed ERMIONI.

1937: Sold to L.B. Delidimitris and M.K. Nicolaides, Piraeus.

25.7.1940: Sunk by British gunfire off Syros whilst on a voyage from Albania to Patmas with a cargo of petrol and lubricating oil and under charter to Italy.

6. FOY 1902-1918

O.N. 116062 354g 91n.
136.4 x 23.9 x 10.0 feet.
C. 2-cyl. by Ross and Duncan, Govan; 69 NHP, 425 IHP, 9 knots.

7.1902: Completed by R. Williamson and Son, Workington (Yard No. 144).

21.7.1902: Registered in the ownership of the Fowey (No. 3) Steamship Co. Ltd. (Toyne, Carter and Co., managers), Fowey as FOY.

12.8.1918: Sold to the Holman Coal and Shipping Co. Ltd. (Frederick W. Holman, manager), Cardiff.

24.11.1927: Sold to the Derwent Steam Shipping Co. Ltd. (Anthony and Bainbridge, managers), Newcastle-upon-Tyne.

31.1.1928: Renamed RAVENSDALE.

27.10.1930: Stranded at Grande Havre Bay, Guernsey whilst on a voyage from Keadby to Jersey with a cargo of slag.

27.10.1930: Abandoned as a total loss.

23.11.1930: Refloated and taken to St. Sampsons, Guernsey.

3.12.1930: Register closed.

2.5.1931: Re-registered in the ownership of the Guernsey Railway Co. Ltd. (Gervase Peek, manager), Guernsey.

1933: Sold to John R. Hird, London.

8.12.1933: Register closed on sale to A. Mannaart, Netherlands and renamed FLEVOMEER.

9.2.1934: Stranded at Nykobing during a voyage from Fredericia to Rotterdam with a cargo of Rye. Refloated and broken up at Rotterdam.

7. EARL CAIRNS 1917-1924 Wooden auxiliary schooner

O.N. 87826 127g 98n.
93.1 x 23.0 x 10.4 feet.
3.1921: 2-cyl. 2SCSA oil engine by the Widdop Engine Company, Keighley; 22 NHP, 80 BHP, 9 knots.

1924: 2-cyl. oil engine by the Invincible Engine Company, Keighley; 22 NHP, 80 BHP, 6 knots.

4.1883: Launched by Ferguson and Baird, Connah's Quay (Yard No. 37).

3.5.1883: Registered in the ownership of George T. Raynes, Liverpool as EARL CAIRNS.

12.3.1891: Transferred to James W. Raynes, Liverpool.

20.7.1907: Sold to William Hancock and Co. (Hawarden) Ltd. (Frederick L. Hancock, manager), Broughton near Chester.

23.1.1917: Sold to Thomas S. Wilson and William Reid, Belfast.

17.7.1917: Acquired by John P. Carter and Charles L. Toyne, Fowey

3.1921: Fitted with auxiliary oil engine.

11.8.1921: Transferred to Toyne, Carter and Co. Ltd., Fowey.

14.8.1924: Sold to George S. Watkins and Wells A. Watkins, Frampton-on-Severn.

1924: Fitted with a new auxiliary oil engine

4.5.1929: Fire in her engine room led to her being condemned as a constructive

The wooden schooner *Earl Cairns* in her later years. *[World Ship Society Ltd.]*

Foy discharging coal with a quayside crane. As her funnel now appears to be black, this may well depict her in the period from 1918 to 1927 when she had been sold Holman Coal and Shipping Co. Ltd. but not renamed. *[Author's collection]*

total loss and abandoned to underwriters.

7.9.1929: Register closed. However, she was duly repaired.

1.11.1929: Re-registered in the ownership of Frederick S. Harris and Sons, Appledore.

20.1.1930: Owners now Sydney G.H. Harris, Percy H. Harris, Sidney Victor Harris and Philip K. Harris, Appledore.

During the Second World War, requisitioned for work with barrage balloons.

19.8.1947: Register closed, unfit for further sea service.

8. A.B. SHERMAN 1921-1923
Four-masted wooden schooner
O.N. 131989 623g 553n.
177.7 x 35.5 x 15.0 feet.

1883: Built by R. Crosbie and Son, East Boston, Massachusetts, U.S.A. for Samuel H. Walker, Taunton, Massachusetts as the three-masted schooner A.B. SHERMAN.

1891: Owner D.H. Walker, Fall River, Massachusetts.

1893: Sold to B.A. Pillsbury, New York, U.S.A.

1900: Sold to Jonathan May and Sons, Philadelphia, Pennsylvania, U.S.A.

26.6.1917: Shelled by the German submarine UC 62 80 miles south west of the Scillies in position 48.03 north, 07.25 west whilst on a voyage from Philadelphia to Le Havre with a cargo of cotton and oil. The U-boat broke off the attack when an armed steamer appeared, but attempted to sink the schooner with scuttling charges on 27. 7.1917. Towed into St. Marys, Scilly Isles, with extensive damage, and later taken to Plymouth.

13.10.1921: After extensive repairs, registered in the ownership of Toyne, Carter and Co. Ltd. (John P. Carter, manager), Fowey as a four-masted schooner.

1.11.1923: Register closed on sale to Raffaello Chiesa, Leghorn, Italy and renamed RAFFAELLO CHIESA.

1932: Deleted from 'Lloyd's Register'.

9. MARY PEERS 1921-1923
Wooden auxiliary schooner
O.N. 67965 149g 97n.
94.8 x 23.5 x 12.0 feet.

1919: Oil engine 2-cyl. by Widdop Engine Company, Keighley; 22 NHP, 70 BHP.

1875: Built by Clemens, Gannel, Newquay for John Peers, Connahs Quay as MARY PEERS.

1885: Sold to Henry Charles Carter, Connah's Quay.

1892: Sold to John Coppack, Connahs Quay.

1896: Sold to John P. Carter, Fowey.

1921: Owners became Toyne, Carter and Co. Ltd. (38/64), John P. Carter (16/64), both Fowey and three other owners on Deeside (10/64).

7.12.1923: Lost near Portwrinkle, Whitsand Bay, Cornwall whilst on a voyage from Torquay to Fowey in ballast. The crew was rescued.

26.2.1924: Register closed.

Mary Peers at Preston in 1921. *Mary Peers* made two visits to Preston in that year arriving on 24th May and 10th September from Charlestown with cargoes of clay. After discharge she went round to the Mersey in ballast. *[World Ship Society Ltd.]*

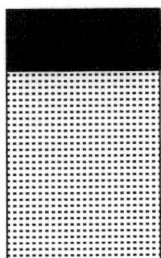

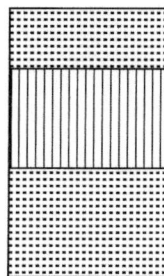

Red   Blue   Yellow or Buff   Green

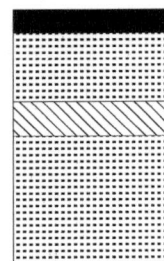

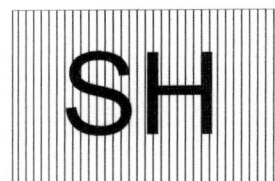

Above: funnel and flag of Toyne, Carter and Co.: letters are red.
Top right: funnels reported for Hannan, Samuel and Co. Ltd. Letters on band may be white or yellow.
Bottom right: Samuel Hough and Co. (Shipping) Ltd. Letters on house flag are white. *[J.L. Loughran]*

The Dutch-built *Polperro* running trials. *[Author's collection]*

Hannan, Samuel and Co. Ltd.

In the very late 1930s a small fleet of motor coasters was managed by Hannan, Samuel and Co. Ltd., Fowey's other major ship broker. Sadly, as with Toyne, Carter, the business was not to prosper.

Hannan, Samuel and Company had been founded about 1884 by a William Francis Hannan, who – like Charles Toyne – was involved in the management of local sailing vessels, including *Concord*, *Wild Wave*, *Maria Luigia* and *Perseverance*. On his death in 1900, his son John Henry Hannan continued the business, eventually in partnership with brother-in-law Sydney J. Samuel, who was also a director of the Fowey Tug Co. Ltd. However, the impetus for entering ship owning appears to have come partly from Stafford Frank Hough, who managed the office of Coast Lines at Falmouth. He was a descendant of Samuel Hough, whose company had, in 1913, merged with others to form Powell, Bacon and Hough Lines Ltd., which four years later became Coast Lines Ltd. Sydney

Samuel and Stafford Hough envisaged a Cornish-owned shipping company, which would trade with china clay to the Baltic, returning with timber.

Initially, the title H. and S. Shipping Co. Ltd. was adopted, and it certainly succeeded in attracting investors from Cornwall. Four orders were eventually placed for motor coasters, three in the Netherlands and one in the United Kingdom, although only two of these were to be delivered to the company. The Dutch orders went to a yard at Foxhol, although sources differ as to its name: the ships' registration papers cite Muller & Broerken, but 'Lloyd's Register' gives N.V. Scheepswerf 'Foxhol', presumably its trading name. *Polperro* was launched in late October 1937, entering service in December. A virtual sister, with minor modifications including a more powerful diesel engine, was then ordered, and was delivered as *Poldhu* in February 1939. The name of the owning company was changed to Polpen Shipping Co. Ltd. in August 1939. A third and slightly larger motor

ship had been ordered from Foxhol, but delivery is said to have been prevented by the outbreak of war, and she was sold to Swedish owners as *Sigbritt*, entering service in March 1940. A fourth motor vessel was reportedly under construction in a British yard, and was requisitioned and completed by the Ministry of War Transport. Its identity has not been established.

War was to continue to have grave effects on the small fleet. When only nine months old, the *Poldhu* went aground near Brest. This was late in May 1940, when the military situation in France was grave; the previous day 'Operation Dynamo' was put into effect to rescue troops facing encirclement at Dunkirk. Hence little could be done to refloat *Poldhu*, although the German occupiers of France soon showed that this was feasible. The career of *Poldhu* under German control is not known to the author, and any information on this would be welcome. *Polperro* had a somewhat longer career, but succumbed in early January 1944 when caught by a German torpedo craft south of Cornwall.

Despite these losses, Hannan, Samuel and Co. Ltd. was not without work. The Ministry of War Transport, and its successor the Ministry of Transport, allocated it an odd collection of vessels for management during the war and for some years after, including two new motor ships, two

Ships managed for the Government by Hanna, Samuel and Co. Ltd.			
Name	**Built/tons**	**Dates**	**Notes**
Empire Punch	1942/321	1942-43	Became *Oakdene*.
Empire Leech	1929/348	1944-46	Dutch motor coaster, ex-*Escaut*.
Empire Fastness	1944/411	1944-46	Became *Firmity*.
Ogre (Balga)	1918/364	1947-53	Dutch-built steam coaster
Alar (aux)	1939/180	1948-51	Estonian wooden auxiliary schooner
Bug	1939/505	1948-49	Polish, Dutch-built motor coaster

Polperro (2) in the Avon. Note her extensive cargo gear and the davits installed amidships. *[Author's collection]*

Dutch-built coasters, and two former Estonian vessels - a steam coaster and a wooden auxiliary schooner. The last-named had been under German control, and tramped around the U.K. under a number of masters who haled from Latvia or Estonia.

After the war there was a modest revival of the fortunes of the Polpen Shipping Co. Ltd., although its management company was soon to sever its connections with Fowey. *Poldhu* was recovered from German hands in May 1945, although it took more than a year for her to be reconditioned and returned to service. In an echo of the anachronism of Toyne, Carter moving from steam to sail, in November 1945 the formerly all-diesel fleet of Polpen acquired its first steamer, the 24-year old *Kenrix* which it renamed *Polkerris*. However, during 1946 management of these two vessels was transferred to Samuel, Hough and Co. (Shipping) Ltd., clearly a company closely related to Hannan, Samuel and Co. Ltd., but which was based in Falmouth. Hannan, Samuel continued to manage a diminishing number of odd vessels for the Ministry of Transport, until 1953.

Despite management being transferred to Falmouth, the Polpen company retained its official place of business in Fowey, and indeed was joined there by a new company, the Trevarth Shipping Co. Ltd. In April

1946, Trevarth acquired its first ship, the steam coaster *Broomlands*, which in July it renamed *Polurrian*, although it was sold just a year later. Another elderly acquisition was the German-built steamer *Empire Constancy*, bought from the Ministry of Transport in 1947 and renamed *Polzeath*. She was transferred to Trevarth Shipping Co. Ltd. in 1948, lasting until 1951. Perhaps surprisingly, and in contrast to the last two acquisitions, in April 1949 a large, brand new motor ship was delivered, the second *Polperro*. Costing £127,000, this was a bold, perhaps too bold, step.

What went wrong for the Polpen company can be pieced together from the increasingly gloomy annual reports sent to shareholders. These have survived through being attached to the company's accounts, deposited with the Registrar of Companies, a good selection of which have been preserved in the National Archives.

Polpen Shipping decided that opportunities lay in trading along the West African coast, although none of its directors seems to have direct experience of working there. The company's capital was duly increased to £125,000, bringing in a growing number of investors from outside Cornwall. During 1948 the motor ship *Poldhu* and, the perhaps less suitable, steamer *Polkerris* were sent out to West Africa, the former incurring

'substantial' costs to make her suitable. But by the end of 1948, losses were already piling up, and continued; the 1949 annual report citing the high cost of operating in West Africa. There was cause for optimism, however, in that the extension of the wharf at Apapa, completed in June 1949, was said to be improving the efficiency of handling of cargo for Lagos, plus there were port improvements at Douala. Shipments paid for by Marshall Aid were expected to greatly increase trade.

But despite these prospects, the total deficit had reached over £46,000 by the end of 1950, and someone had to be found to take the blame. This fell on managers Samuel, Hough and Co. (Shipping) Ltd., and as a result Samuel and John S. Hough both resigned from the Polpen board and their company's management contract with Polpen was terminated at the end of 1950. Much of the money owed by this company to Polpen was deemed irrecoverable and was written off, although threats of legal action rumbled on for years.

Efforts to improve Polpen's situation included recruiting new board members with shipping industry experience, which probably necessitated the relocation of the registered office to London in May 1951. Fresh blood included a new chairman who had West African connections whilst another manager spent much time on the African coast trying to sort out problems. He found that surveys were taking an unduly long time; on *Poldhu* loadline surveys took four months, whilst *Polkerris* was laid up for five months whilst surveys were done by Lloyd's Register. The previous managers provided a useful scapegoat for the steamer's poor condition which caused the delays. Trading conditions actually deteriorated towards the end of 1952, as the oil companies active in Nigeria changed their distribution arrangements with bulk storage facilities being provided so that fewer drums were being shipped. To make matters worse, increasing competition was being felt from Dutch, German and even French coasters, and ballast passages became more numerous. Perhaps not surprisingly, the master of *Poldhu* suffered a nervous breakdown during 1953, whilst her second engineer was hospitalised, leaving the ship idle for six weeks whist replacements were sent out.

It was decided to bring home first the *Polkerris* and later the *Poldhu*, but even this operation was fraught, necessitating the expense of running crews. On arrival, *Polkerris* was sold for scrap. *Poldhu* soldiered on in West Africa until the frequency of her ballast passages in 1954 and her need for

Fleet list: Hannan, Samuel and Co. Ltd., Fowey
H. and S. Shipping Co. Ltd
Polpen Shipping Co. Ltd.

1. POLPERRO (1) 1938-1944
O.N. 164247 403g 204n.
145.6 x 26.0 x 9.1 feet.
Oil engine 4SCSA 6-cyl. by Appingedammer Bronsmotorenfabriek, Appingedam, Netherlands; 76 NHP, 430 IHP, 360 BHP, 8.5 knots
30.10.1937: Launched by N.V. Scheepswerf 'Foxhol', Foxhol, Netherlands (Yard No. 45).
12.1937: Completed.
1.1.1938: Registered in the ownership of H. and S. Shipping Co. Ltd. (Hannan, Samuel and Co. Ltd., managers), Fowey as POLPERRO.
28.8.1939: Owners became Polpen Shipping Co. Ltd. (Hannan, Samuel and Co. Ltd., managers), Fowey.
6.1.1944: Torpedoed and sunk by a boat of the German fifth S.-Flottile in position 49.57 north, 05.38 west whilst

repairs brought her home, arriving on the Tyne in May 1955. Special survey revealed that she needed £25,000 to put her right, and so it was decided to sell her. She fetched just £7,650 on sale to W.N. Lindsay Ltd. of Leith, who after repairs traded her for another ten years.

The second *Polperro* presents something of a mystery. Why did a company, relying otherwise on second-hand tonnage, splash out so much on a sophisticated new ship? The photograph of her in the Avon in September 1949 shows her with davits between holds two and three, to accommodate boats and suggesting she was to carry deck passengers. She also has extensive cargo gear, suggesting she was intended for some sort of liner service. She may well have been designed for West African services, but if so the photograph shows that within five months of her delivery in April 1949 she was in the home trade, confirmed by an annual report of her owners. Financial losses that year prompted her disposal, and she arrived at Rotterdam on 24th January 1950, then proceeded to London for docking and inspection prior to sale, on which a loss of almost £18,000 was recorded. The annual report recording that her sale was made 'at some sacrifice', may have been economical with the truth, as there

on a voyage from Manchester and Milford Haven to Penryn with a cargo of coal.
31.1.1944: Register closed.

2. POLDHU 1939-1940, 1946-1956
O.N. 164250 410g 193n.
145.7 x 26.0 x 9.1 feet.
Oil engine 4SCSA 6-cyl. by Appingedammer Bronsmotorenfabriek, Appingedam, Netherlands; 76 NHP, 432 IHP, 360 BHP, 8.5 knots.
2.1939: Completed by N.V. Scheepswerf 'Foxhol', Foxhol, Netherlands (Yard No. 49).
23.2.1939: Registered in the ownership of H. and S. Shipping Co. Ltd. (Hannan, Samuel and Co. Ltd., managers), Fowey as POLDHU.
28.8.1939: Owners became Polpen Shipping Co. Ltd. (Hannan, Samuel and Co. Ltd., managers), Fowey.
27.5.1940: Wrecked south west of Ile de Sein near Brest whilst on a voyage from Oporto to Jersey with a cargo of boxboard.
12.9.1940: Register closed.

is evidence that her sale, in December 1950, was at the behest of the Admiralty Marshall.

Following the sale of *Poldhu* in 1955 it was concluded that resources were quite inadequate to replace her, and the best hope was that someone might purchase the Polpen Shipping Co. Ltd. It was not until July 1957 that the directors faced the inevitable and decided to wind up a company whose deficits now totalled over £76,000. It had been a sorry tale of a previously modest company considerably over-reaching itself. It is perhaps some consolation for the Cornish that the painful demise of Polpen Shipping and its various owners and managers happened a long way away, initially in West Africa where conditions meant that management was out of its depth, and finally in the City of London where, despite the efforts of the great and the good of the shipping industry, the company could not be rescued from ever deeper ignominy.

Despite the efforts of Toyne, Carter and Hannan, Samuel, during the powered ship era Fowey could not emulate its success in sailing vessel days as a port in which coastal ships were successfully built and owned.

7.1940: Refloated during the German occupation.
5.1945: Recovered.
22.6.1946: Re-registered in the ownership of Polpen Shipping Co. Ltd. (Hannan, Samuel and Co. Ltd., managers), Fowey.
1946: Managers became Samuel, Hough and Co. (Shipping) Ltd., Falmouth.
30.12.1950: Management terminated.
1955: Managers became Purvis Shipping Co. Ltd.
1.1956: Sold to W.N. Lindsay Ltd., Leith and renamed ROSELYNE.
8.1966: Sold to Nicholas Barbas and Dimitrios Moschovis, Thessaloniki, Greece and renamed ANNA.
1972: Sold to Anna Iakovou Kalligeraki, Panama.
1976: Sold to Marisud S.p.A., Augusta, Italy and renamed ELEUSI.
1981: Sold to Angelo Spinelli, Brindisi, Italy.
5.1997: Deleted from 'Lloyd's Register' as continued existence in doubt.

Poldhu in the Thames in 1955. *[T. Rayner/J. and M. Clarkson]*

3. POLKERRIS 1945-1953
O.N. 144079 692g 317n.
175.0 x 29.1 x 11.3 feet.
T. 3-cyl. by John Lewis and Sons Ltd.,
Aberdeen; 96 NHP, 600 IHP, 9 knots.
5.1921: Completed by Cochrane and
Sons Ltd., Selby (Yard No.701).
20.7.1921: Registered in the ownership
of Robert Rix and Sons, Hull as
KENRIX.
23.11.1945: Sold to the Polpen Shipping
Co. Ltd. (Hannan, Samuel and Co. Ltd.,
managers), Fowey.
4.2.1946: Renamed POLKERRIS.
1946: Managers became Samuel,
Hough and Co. (Shipping) Ltd.,
Falmouth.
30.12.1950: Management terminated.
31.12.1953: Arrived at Dunston-on-
Tyne for breaking up by C.W. Dorkin
and Co. Ltd.
14.6.1954: Register closed

4. POLZEATH 1947-1951
O.N. 180639 535g 268n.
166.5 x 28.6 x 11.5 feet.
C. 2-cyl. by Stettiner Oderwerke A.G.,
Stettin, Germany.
3.10.1912: Launched by Stettiner
Oderwerke A.G., Stettin (Yard No. 640).
2.11.1912: Completed for Vereinigte
Bugsir und Frachtschiffahrt Gesellschaft
A.G., Hamburg, Germany as
DOLLART.
1.5.1919: Transferred to Bugsier
Reederei und Bergungs A.G., Hamburg.
18.5.1945: Found by Allied forces at
Copenhagen.
27.6.1945: Delivered to Methil.

1945: Registered in the ownership
of the Ministry of Transport, London
(Thomas Rose and Co., Sunderland,
managers) as EMPIRE CONSTANCY.
1.4.1946: Owner became the Ministry
of Transport, London.
1947: Acquired by the Polpen Shipping
Co. Ltd. (Samuel Hough and Co.
(Shipping), Ltd., Falmouth, managers)
and renamed POLZEATH.
1948: Transferred to the Trevarth
Shipping Co. Ltd., Fowey (Samuel
Hough and Co. (Shipping) Ltd.,
Falmouth, managers).
1951: Sold to Azize Arkan ve Ortaklari,
Istanbul, Turkey and renamed
MELTEM.
1956: Renamed YENER.
1959: Sold to Erpak Co. Ltd.
1961: Sold to Zeki ve Ziya Sonmez
Izzet Kirtil, Istanbul and renamed
YARASLI.

14.1.1961: Left Istanbul for Bagnoli
with a cargo of scrap iron and went
missing after passing Cephalonia
25.1.1961.

5. POLPERRO (2) 1949-1950
O.N. 183331 1,130g 597n.
215.5 x 34.2 x 11.9 feet.
2SCSA 6-cyl. oil engine by British Polar
Engines Ltd., Glasgow; 1,000 BHP.
10.8.1948: Launched by Charles Hill
and Sons Ltd., Bristol (Yard No. 352).
4.1949: Completed for Polpen Shipping
Co. Ltd., Fowey (Samuel Hough
and Co. (Shipping) Ltd., Falmouth,
managers) at a cost of £127,000 as
POLPERRO.
12.1950: Sold to Galbraith, Pembroke
and Co. Ltd., London for £110,000 by
the Admiralty Marshal, and bare-boat
chartered to Ben Line Steamers Ltd. to
operate a service between Singapore

The German steamer *Dollart* pre-war. She became *Polzeath*. *[Schiffsfoto Jansen]*

and Bangkok, registered at Leith and renamed BENVEG.

9.1951: Sold to Ben Line Steamers Ltd., Leith.

9.1951: Sold to James Fisher and Sons Ltd., Barrow-in-Furness and renamed SOUND FISHER.

13.1.1957: Foundered five miles east of Noss Head, Caithness, while on passage from Lyness, Orkney to Ghent, Belgium. A heavy list developed after her cargo of scrap iron had shifted and, although taken in tow, she capsized and sank. Her crew of seven was rescued by fishing vessels and landed at Wick.

Trevarth Shipping Co. Ltd., Fowey

1. POLURRIAN 1946-1947

O.N. 145094 518g 284n.
157.7 x 26.2 x 12.1 feet.
T. 3-cyl. by William Beardmore and Co. Ltd., Coatbridge, Glasgow; 77 NHP, 450 IHP, 9 knots.

1957: Oil engine 6-cyl. by Waggon und Maschinenbau, Gorlitz, West Germany.

3.6.1920: Launched by Swan, Hunter and Wigham Richardson Ltd., Wallsend-on-Tyne (Yard No. 1149).

15.11.1920: Registered in the ownership of Harold Harrison, London as ALFRED HARRISON.

16.11.1920: Completed.

23.8.1921: Owners became H. Harrison (Shipping) Ltd., London.

28.2.1930: Sold to Albert Chester (32/64) and Edwin G. Tyerman (32/64), Middlesbrough.

30.4.1930: Renamed BROOMLANDS.

18.4.1946: Sold to Trevarth Shipping Co. Ltd., Fowey (Samuel, Hough and Co. (Shipping) Ltd., Falmouth, managers).

10.7.1946: Renamed POLURRIAN.

24.7.1947: Sold to Oddson and Co. Ltd., Hull.

1947: Renamed RIFSNES.

4.1.1952: Sold to Risted and Nerdrum Ltd., London.

25.4.1952: Renamed ARILD.

26.10.1954: Owners became Nerdrum Shipping Ltd., London. In 1954 it was intended to rename her NORBURY, but this was not carried out.

5.1955: Sold to Raphael Melachrinos and Sons and Elias Tomboulis, Piraeus, Greece and renamed ASPASIA.

Arild, formerly Polurrian. [Author's collection]

1957: Fitted with new oil engine.

1958: Owner became Raphael D. Melachrinos and Co., Piraeus.

1961: Sold to Evangelos Tsitsilicas and Co., Thessalonika, Greece and renamed MARILENA.

1971: Broken up in Greece.

2. POLZEATH 1948-1951

See Polpen Shipping Co. Ltd. number 4.

Managed for the Ministry of War Transport/Ministry of Transport, London

1. EMPIRE PUNCH 1942-1943

O.N. 166691 321g 145n.
137.0 (o.a.) 131.5 x 24.6 x 8.8 feet.
Oil engine 2SCSA 6-cyl. by Crossley Brothers Ltd., Manchester; 116 NHP.

5.1942: Completed by Richards Ironworks Ltd., Lowestoft (Yard No. 296).

29.5.1942: Registered in the ownership of the Ministry of War Transport, London (Hannan, Samuel and Co. Ltd., Fowey, managers) as EMPIRE PUNCH.

2.1943: Managers became Argosies Ltd., London.

1.4.1946: Owner became the Ministry of Transport, London.

18.1.1947: Sold to Lovering and Sons Ltd., Cardiff

1955: Sold to T.G. Irving Ltd. (T.G. Irving, manager), Sunderland and renamed OAKDENE.

1967: Sold to George I.F. and Evar C.D. Sealy, St. Michael, Barbados.

1993: Deleted from 'Lloyd's Register' as continued existence in doubt.

2. EMPIRE LEECH 1944-1946

O.N. 169857 363g 217n.
145.0 x 24.5 x 9.9 feet.
Oil engine 2SCSA 6-cyl. by Motorenfabrik 'Deutz' A.G., Koln-Deutz, Germany; 70 NHP, 7 knots.

12.1929: Completed by N.V. Scheepswerf v. J. Smit Czn., Alblasserdam, Netherlands (Yard No. 506) for N.V. W.H. Müller & Co's. Erts en Scheepvaart Bedrijf, Rotterdam, Netherlands as ESCAUT.

1932: Transferred to W.H. Müller & Co. N.V., Rotterdam

Oakdene, ex-Empire Punch. [World Ship Society Ltd.]

Seine, the former *Empire Leech*, in the Thames 8th August 1953. *[V.H.Young & L.A.Sawyer]*

25.3.1941: Heavily damaged by German air attack near Crackington Haven. Beached and, although declared a constructive total loss, refloated and repaired.

5.5.1944: Registered in the ownership of the Ministry of War Transport, London (Hannan, Samuel and Co. Ltd., Fowey, managers) as EMPIRE LEECH.

20.3.1946: Owner became the Ministry of Transport, London.

8.8.1946: Managers became the Adriatic Steam Ship Co. Ltd.

8.8.1947: Sold to the Adriatic Steam Ship Co. Ltd. (Horace S. Cordran, manager), London.

9.6.1948: Sold to the Vianda Steam Ship Co. Ltd. (Wm. H. Müller and Co. (London) Ltd., managers), London.

6.9.1948: Renamed SEINE.

16.7.1955: Sunk following a collision in fog with the U.S.S.R. motor tanker DROGOBITZ (3,100/1954) six miles off Dungeness whilst on a voyage from Paris to London.

1.9.1955: Register closed.

3. EMPIRE FASTNESS 1944-1946
O.N. 180325   411g 190n.
142.2 x 27.0 x 8.50 feet.
6-cyl. 2SCSA oil engine by British Polar Engines Ltd., Glasgow; 8 knots.
10.1952: 6-cyl 2SCSA oil engine by Newbury Diesel Co. Ltd., Newbury.

5.12.1944: Completed by Henry Scarr Ltd., Hessle (Yard No. S456) for the Ministry of War Transport, London (Hannan, Samuel and Co. Ltd., Fowey, managers) as EMPIRE FASTNESS. She was originally to be named FABRIC 47.

1.4.1946: Owner became the Ministry of Transport, London.

23.9.1946: Sold to F.T. Everard and Sons Ltd., Greenhithe.

4.12.1946: Renamed FIRMITY.

10.1952: Re-engined.

17.3.1964: Sold to A.E. Pierce, Canvey Island.

9.1964: Sold to Metaal Handel & Sloopwerken H.P. Heuvelman for demolition at Krimpen aan den IJssel, Netherlands.

12.1964: Demolition completed.

4. OGRE 1947-1953
O.N. 139638   364g 176n.
132.4 x 23.3 x 10.3 feet.
T. 3-cyl. by H. Versteig, Neder Hardingsveld, Netherlands.
1918: Completed by Gebroeders van der Windt, Vlaardingen, Netherlands (Yard No. 207) for N.V. Vrachtvaarts Nereus (A. Jordens, junior, manager), Rotterdam, Netherlands as NAUTILUS.

12.9.1919: Sold to the Nuorla Steam Ship Co. Ltd. (William Stuart, manager), Cardiff and renamed NUORLA.

13.9.1919: Sold to Harold Harrison and Edward T. Lindley, London.

20.10.1919: Transferred to the Horley Steam Ship Co. Ltd. (Harold Harrison, manager), London.

Everard's *Firmity* began life as *Empire Fastness* under Hannan, Samuel management. *[J. and M. Clarkson]*

Ogre she was managed post-war by Hannan, Samuel on behalf of the Ministry of Transport. *[Author's collection]*

12.12.1919: Acquired by Richard P. Care, Cardiff.

12.2.1920: Sold to the Anglo-American Oil Co. Ltd. (James Hamilton, manager), London.

3.12.1931: Manager became Frederick J. Wolfe.

26.10.1936: Sold to Borge Bentzen, Copenhagen, Denmark and renamed SELMA B.

1939: Sold to Kopredereja 'Ogre' (J. Sausins, manager), Riga, Latvia and renamed OGRE.

1940: Transferred to J. Sausins, Riga.

1940: Sold to Liepajas Drasu Fabrika, Liepaja, Latvia.

6.1940: Seized by the U.S.S.R. in Baltic waters.

10.1940: Formally expropriated and transferred to Latviyskoye gosudarstvyennoye morskoye parokhodstvo, Riga, Russia.

30.6.1941: Captured by German troops at Libau and transferred to ownership of Deutsches Reich as the Kriegsmarine transport BALGA.

1942: Converted to a buoy tender.

5.1945: Taken by Allied forces at Rendsburg.

1947: Transferred to the Ministry of Transport, London (Hannan, Samuel and Co. Ltd., Fowey, managers) as OGRE.

1947: Proposed to rename her BALGA, but – although briefly listed as this in 'Lloyd's Register' – this was never officially carried out.

26.8.1953: Sailed Fowey for Llanelly.

26.10.1953: Breaking up began by the Rees Shipbreaking Co. Ltd., Llanelly.

21.1.1954: Register closed.

5. ALAR 1948-1951 Wooden auxiliary three-masted schooner

O.N. 181909 180g 133n.
102.3 x 23.7 x 9.6 feet.
Oil engine 2SCSA 2-cyl. by J. & C.G. Bolinders M.V. A/B, Stockholm, Sweden; 62 NHP, 120 BHP, 7 knots.

1939: Completed by P. Himmist, Hiiuman Island, Estonia for M. Markson, M. Türi and others, Tallinn, Estonia as ALAR.

c 1940-1945: Under German control as KURLAND.

7.5.1948: Registered in the ownership of the Ministry of Transport, London (Hannan, Samuel and Co. Ltd., Fowey, managers).

18.1.1951: Register closed on sale to owners registered in Costa Rica..

6. BUG 1948-1949

O.N. 169830 505g 303n.
(168.5 o.a.) 158.5 x 27.4 x 9.7 feet.
Oil engine 4SDSA 8-cyl. by Humboldt Deutzmotoren A.G., Koln-Deutz, Germany; 94 NHP, 10 knots

8.1939: Completed by N.V. E.J. Smit & Zonen Scheepswerf, Westerbroek, Netherlands (Yard No. 660) for Rothert and Kilaczyki Ltd. (R. Kilaczycki, manager), Gdynia, Poland as BUG.

7.4.1944: Registered in the ownership of the Ministry of War Transport, London (Pinch and Simpson, managers), London.

20.3.1946: Owner became the Ministry of Transport, London.

6.1.1948: Managers became Hannan, Samuel and Co. Ltd., Fowey.

6.11.1949: Register closed on transfer to Zegluga Polska, S.A., Gdynia, Poland.

1951: Transferred to Polskie Linie Oceaniczne, Szczecin, Poland.

1960: Transferred to Polska Zegluga Morska, Szczecin

24.4.1964: Breaking up began at Gdansk.

The Dutch-built *Bug* back under the Polish flag post-war. Was the block on her boat deck built to house DEMS gunners? *[Dave Hocquard]*

174

A FOY BOAT
Captain A.W. Kinghorn

Clinker-built wooden craft like this were used to take mooring lines from ships, so called because in the days of sail the foyboatmen would head out to sea to meet an incoming vessel and arrange with its master a fee ('foy') for their services. They would then put a line aboard the ship and be towed in towards the harbour where, at the designated berth, they made her fast with the number of lines ordered by the master.

Usually two or three men crewed the foy boat. Some put out to sea, under a lugsail, others like Alfred Dunmore of Tyne Dock, worked exclusively in rivers or docks, in his case the Tyne, Northumberland and Albert Edward Dock, where their job was regular if less lucrative.

Foy boats on the Tyne were always painted green inboard. The black 'gun ports' on the white strake were actually protruding wooden fenders to protect the boat when alongside a ship. With no engines, they were rowed or more often sculled with a single oar over the stern.

In the Tyne's heyday, a number of foy boats could be seen moored in the downriver water sheltered from the wash of the river traffic near South Shields ferry landing.

RECORD REVIEW

A SAILOR'S LIFE: The life and times of John Short of Watchet 1839-1933
Tom Brown
Softback 21 x 14.7 cms of 166 pages
Published by S&A Projects at £12.00

This is undoubtedly an unusual book to be reviewed in 'Record'. It is about a sailor and not ships, has very few illustrations of ships, and is definitely the first book we have reviewed with pages devoted to words and music. Yet it is an impressive and important piece of work, the research for which would not disgrace a highly experienced maritime historian.

John Short was in all but one respects a typical seaman of the age of sail (his one voyage under steam ended in an accident). His claim to fame and his significance aboard ships was that he was a talented shantyman, and he became a major source for that doyen of folk song collectors of the 20th century, Cecil Sharp. The many shanties remembered by Short and written down by Sharp have added significantly to our knowledge of these songs and the important part they played in working sailing ships. They also comprise a significant part of the repertoire of singers who continue to perform these simple, rousing and often somewhat earthy songs.

Folklorist Dr Tom Brown has strived very hard to compile a complete record of John Short's long career as a seaman, a far from easy task as Short's discharge book has been lost. Working with crew lists (a difficult source as they are very dispersed), plus shipping and local papers, he has traced Short's voyages in detail, and gives brief but satisfyingly accurate biographies of each ship in which he served.

Although the book is likely to appeal most to those who study or sing shanties, it is also a very worthwhile piece of maritime history. There are many accounts of ships' officers' careers, but few if any books recount the life and times of a typical seaman from the age of merchant sail like John Short. Well written, nicely produced and very competitively priced, this book is a little gem.

Roy Fenton

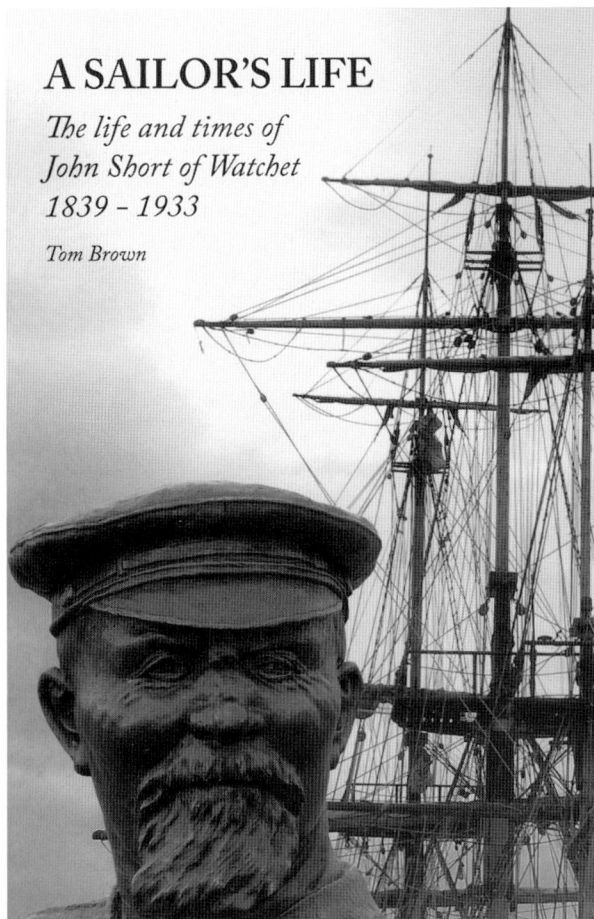

A SAILOR'S LIFE
The life and times of John Short of Watchet 1839 – 1933

Tom Brown

ABERDEEN'S SCRATCHER TRAWLERS
Peter Myers

One of my most evocative memories of Aberdeen from about 40 years ago was watching, from the Beach Esplanade, some of the port's trawlers putting to sea on a Monday morning in the summer. Their masts could be followed filing past the North Pier and as they emerged out into Aberdeen Bay the knowledgeable watcher could identify the ownership of a trawler by her hull and funnel colours. Upon reaching the open water, the trawlers fanned out and headed for the fishing grounds: some for the Faroe Islands, others for the Shetland or west-side grounds while the boats which fished the near waters, known locally as scratchers, set course for the grounds off the Aberdeenshire coast.

The scratchers didn't enjoy the celebrity status of Aberdeen's top-grossing trawlers which usually fished off Faroe and Iceland and in the White Sea, but the short duration of their trips meant their fish was better preserved and sold for higher prices than catches landed by the bigger boats. The humble haddock was the foundation of Aberdeen's fishing prosperity and, although a wide variety of fish was landed, the port handled more haddock than any other species.

In the steam trawling era, the scratchers put to sea once or twice a week and their favoured grounds were the Aberdeen Bank, Buchan Deeps and Turbot Bank, although some ventured as far as the Devil's Hole, 120 miles south east of Aberdeen. They traditionally returned in time to land their catches for the Saturday morning market and sailed again for the fishing grounds on Monday morning. As they were in port over the weekend, the scratchers were also known locally as 'Sunday boaties'. In the early 1950s it was estimated there were about 90 scratchers fishing out of Aberdeen.

Elderly coal-burning steam trawlers were predominant among Aberdeen's scratchers in the late 1940s and 1950s. In 1950, out of 196 operational trawlers at the port, 173 were over 25 years old, 11 over 20 years, and only eight under 10 years of age. The many small firms owning less than five vessels did not have the financial resources to invest in new

The *Annabelle*, owned by D. Wood of Aberdeen, was built by Hall, Russell in 1917 as the Strath class Admiralty trawler *George Borthwick*, and lasted until 1960 when she was scrapped. She is shown passing Pocra Quay at Aberdeen where a Bangor class minesweeper is berthed. *[Peter Myers collection]*

diesel- or oil-fired steam trawlers and it was left to the larger companies, such as Richard Irvin and Sons Ltd. and the Walker Steam Trawl Fishing Co. Ltd., to order new vessels.

Life on the trawlers

Retired skipper Alfie Freeland gave me an insight into life on the steam trawlers and his 43-year career in trawling when I visited him at his Aberdeen home in 1979. He had first gone to sea as a deckhand in 1917 at the age of 17, and four years later obtained his mate's ticket. After a further six years he successfully sat for his skipper's ticket. Mr Freeland skippered five steam trawlers and, in order of command, they were the *Strathella*, *Glenogil*, *Sylverdyke*, *Bervie Braes* and *Agnes Nutten*. He told me that the skipper and mate did not receive a fixed wage, and instead their remuneration was on the basis of poundage. A catch which grossed £100 at the fish market would yield the skipper £10 and the mate £8. The expenses of trawling, including the crew's wages, bunker coal, insurance

The steam trawler *Bracondene*, built by Alexander Hall and Co. Ltd., Aberdeen, in 1916, passes the harbour's Torry Dock where some of the port's new motor trawlers are gathered, many of which were built at John Lewis and Sons' shipyard at Torry, right. *[World Ship Society Ltd.]*

The long-lived *Bervie Braes* was built as the Strath class Admiralty trawler *George Burton* by Hall, Russell in 1917. With staysail set she is shown passing the *St Clement* of the North of Scotland, Orkney and Shetland Shipping Co. Ltd. at Matthews Quay while outbound from Aberdeen circa 1959. *[World Ship Society Ltd.]*

and dock charges were deducted from the 'gross' amount. A poor catch yielding a low 'gross' meant that both the skipper and mate had to deny themselves wages after the deduction of all expenses.

Before sailing for the fishing grounds a scratcher would take on five tons of flake ice for preserving the catch and an average of 20 tons of bunker coal, of which extra quantities were stowed in bags around the poop deck. A retired coasting master once told me that they always knew when they were nearing Aberdeen because the port was obscured by a cloud of funnel smoke issuing from steam trawlers preparing to put to sea, and it's not surprising that local fishermen referred to them as 'Smokey Joes'.

Mr Freeland said that poor quality coal often led to a drop in steam pressure resulting in the net being torn because of the ultra slow speed. He added that low steam pressures sometimes caused the skipper and the chief engineer to be at loggerheads, and on more than one occasion Mr Freeland had to make a premature return to port because of low quality coal. He said that after 1945 bunker coal had become more expensive and supplies of good steam coal from the Northumberland and Durham coalfields could not always be relied upon. A mechanical coal-bunkering installation was erected at Point Law at Aberdeen harbour, but the tradition continued of scratch crews

taking trawlers to load bunkers at the Firth of Forth ports of Granton and Methil. By the mid-1950s the coal burners' fuel costs were said to be twice as much as the new motor trawlers for the same trip.

Mr Freeland held the old steam trawlers in high regard and, in his opinion, these well-built vessels could ride out storms better than the modern near-water trawlers built in the 1970s. A less flattering description of the Aberdeen scratchers can be found in Burns Singer's book 'Living Silver, an impression of the British fishing industry', published in 1957. He dismissed them as 'uncomfortable, dangerous, inefficient ships that threatened continually to ruin their owners and drown their crews' but nonetheless admitted that 'these ancient sea-bitten junk heaps were still helping to make Aberdeen a prosperous city'. It was a view shared by others including an Aberdeen skipper who was quoted in 'The Third Statistical Account of the City of Aberdeen' (1953). He said he would refuse to put to sea in any of these small, obsolescent trawlers, adding: 'They are ill-equipped, they have poor and often scandalous provision for the crews, and sometimes they are rat-infested.'

Long-lived
Some of the scratchers had astonishingly long careers despite these negative comments. The *Bervie*

Braes, among whose skippers was Alfie Freeland, lasted from 1917 until she was sold for demolition in December 1959. She had been completed as the Strath class Admiralty trawler *George Burton* at the Aberdeen yard of Hall, Russell and Co. Ltd. The prototype vessel for the Strath class was the *Strathlochy*, built by Hall, Russell for Aberdeen owners in 1916. Like many of the Straths, the *George Burton* was sold out commercially after the First World War and was renamed *Bervie Braes* (A.883) in 1922. She had a succession of Aberdeen owners, the last of whom was W.J. Fishing Co. Ltd. managed by John Walker. She was bought by Aberdeen shipbuilder John Lewis and Sons Ltd., along with a number of other redundant coal-burners, before being re-sold to firms such as the British Iron and Steel Corporation. Most of the steam trawlers bought by Lewis were broken up at its newly acquired subsidiary yard at Montrose. In the Second World War the *Bervie Braes* was requisitioned by the Admiralty in November 1939 and served as an auxiliary patrol vessel, a minesweeper and a fuel carrier. For the latter role she was fitted with a 33-ton tank for refuelling diesel-driven landing craft and was one of 32 Aberdeen trawlers involved in the D-day landings in June 1944.

Another long-lived scratcher was the *Morven*, which had been built in 1902 by John Duthie, Sons and Co., Aberdeen. She was requisitioned

The veteran scratcher *Morven* of 1902 was the oldest trawler fishing out of Aberdeen in the late 1950s. In the background are the shipyards at Footdee where many of Aberdeen's steam trawlers were built. *[Aberdeen City Libraries]*

by the Admiralty and served in the Dardanelles. Norman Wilkinson, who was an official war artist during the Dardanelles campaign, extolled the trawlers' versatility and said they were 'used for every conceivable kind of work. They have carried stores, troops, mails and munitions. They have been engaged in minesweeping, patrolling and towing nets. They have tackled the elusive submarine'. John Graham, of Aberdeen, bought the *Morven* (A.567) in 1920 and owned her until his son, Charles, took her over in November 1950. She was indisputably the oldest coal-burning steam trawler in the Aberdeen fleet in the late 1950s and was said to be still capable of earning her keep. Her last skipper before she was sold for demolition in August 1960 was James Gatt.

New boats, new operators

However, time was running out for the 'Smokey Joes' as they were being replaced steadily by new motor trawlers, many of which were built under the White Fish Authority's grant-and-loan scheme. By early 1960 the steam trawlers were being withdrawn with some rapidity including 10 during the last week of March.

The Aberdeen fleet's new boats showed their superiority with their more powerful diesel engines and winches, better deck lighting, improved protection for those working on deck and superior accommodation aft for the crew. John Lewis and Sons, whose yard

was on the south side of the harbour at Torry, was kept busy building motor trawlers for the local fleet from the mid-1950s. In 1959 the yard launched no fewer than 11 trawlers into the River Dee.

A new company, Aberdeen Near Water Trawlers Ltd., was set up to operate new diesel-engined scratchers and have them managed by the Don Fishing Co. Ltd. It was a sister company to Aberdeen Motor Trawlers Ltd., which had been formed by fish merchants at the port in 1955 and chaired by Byron Bellamy who was also chairman of the new firm. The company's first boat was the 109-foot

Balnagask (A.294) which landed her first catch at Aberdeen in the autumn of 1959. She had been built by the yard of Cook, Welton and Gemmell Ltd. at Beverley and was followed from the same builder by the 102-foot *Hazlehead* (A.364) which ran her trials in November 1959. The *Hazlehead*'s wheelhouse was fitted with a Brown Bloctube central control console, which incorporated a range of sophisticated steering aids, being among the most advanced in the British trawling fleet at the time. The two Humberside-built trawlers were joined by the *Woodside* (A.365) and the *Countesswells* (A.366) which were built by Alexander Hall and Co. Ltd., Aberdeen in 1959 and 1960 respectively.

Some of the veteran steam scratchers had their lives prolonged by conversion to diesel propulsion. Among them was the *Doreen Johnston* which was renamed *George R. Wood* (A.723) in 1960 after a six-cylinder diesel was fitted. She had been built as the Strath class Admiralty trawler *William Gillett* in 1919 by Ritchie, Graham and Milne of Whiteinch, Glasgow. She later served the Air Ministry as the *Adastral* and during the Second World War was used as a barrage balloon defence ship. Granton owners bought her in 1946 and renamed her *Doreen Johnston* before George Wood (Aberdeen) Ltd. acquired her in 1953. Five years later she came to the help of the motor trawler *Boston Sea Hawk* (A.117), which had developed engine trouble while fishing off Rattray Head, Aberdeenshire, and towed her to Aberdeen.

The Clyde-built *George R. Wood* (1) of 1919 was originally a Strath class Admiralty steam trawler and was re-engined with a diesel in 1960, extending her fishing career by a further 10 years. She is shown leaving Aberdeen in December 1967 on her last fishing trip of the year. *[Aberdeen Journals Ltd.]*

The *George R. Wood* (2), of George Wood (Aberdeen) Ltd., leaving Aberdeen on 28th June 1976, was formerly the *Netherley*, built at Montrose in 1960. *[J. and M. Clarkson]*

George Wood's fleet

George Wood was probably the best-remembered operator of scratchers during the motor trawler era at Aberdeen and its managed companies included the Ailsa Craig Fishing Co. Ltd. and the Wilronwood Fishing Co. Ltd. Its trawlers were distinguished by their cream funnels with a black top separated by a narrow red band and green hulls with red boot-topping.

Another veteran in the George Wood fleet was the *Silver Seas* (A.65), which had been built as a steamer for the herring fishery by Cochrane and Sons Ltd., Selby in 1931 for A.G. Catchpole of Lowestoft. Wood bought her in 1960 and converted her to motor propulsion. The 107-ton *Lord Rodney* (A.50) was another former Lowestoft steam drifter to be fitted with a diesel engine after she had been bought by Craigwood Ltd., Aberdeen (George R. Wood, manager) in April 1959. The conversion work also involved removing the herring hatches and installing trawler hatches and a fish room. She had been built by the Goole Shipbuilding and Repairing Co. Ltd., Goole in 1928 and fished out of Aberdeen until sold to Swansea owners in 1967.

It would be unfair to suggest that the George Wood fleet had an elderly profile because the firm's newest vessel was the *Netherley*, built in 1960 by John Lewis's yard at Montrose for the Glendee Fishing Co. Ltd. The 1919-built *George R. Wood* was laid up in 1970 and her name was given to the *Netherley* while the veteran became the new *Netherley*. It was under this name that the old-timer, reported to be Scotland's oldest trawler, sailed from

Aberdeen for the last time on 16th March 1971 bound for the breaker's yard at Bo'ness while towing the *Silver Seas*, also destined to be scrapped.

The George Wood fleet was managed by the old-established Aberdeen firm of Thomas Davidson (Trawlers) Ltd. There was a long association between Davidson and the Wilson family of Portknockie, Banffshire, and skipper George Wilson of the *George R. Wood* (2) had been connected with the firm for many years. His brothers, James and John, were also skippers of Davidson-managed trawlers, while another brother, Joseph, was skipper and part-owner of the *Vigilance*. The Wilson brothers fished the rough and difficult grounds off the Aberdeenshire coast and supplied the market with first-class sole, plaice, haddock, whiting and codling.

Pocket trawlers

In 1968 John Lewis built its first 86-foot pocket trawler, the *Spinningdale* (A.473), for Bruce's Stores Ltd. of Aberdeen. She was a development of the 67 foot 6 inch sputnik trawlers of 48 gross tons built in 1960-62 by John Lewis's yard at Montrose, formerly owned by the Montrose Shipbuilding and Engineering Co. Ltd. and which had been taken over by Lewis in 1959. Lewis had a full order book and its new pocket trawler design was sub-contracted to the Montrose yard at Rossie Island. At least 11 were built for Aberdeen owners while a further 13 sputniks came from the Fairmile Construction Co. Ltd., Berwick-upon-Tweed. The sputniks performed well in the early 1960s before the industry fell into a nationwide depression and which led to an exodus of the type from Aberdeen to other ports during the mid-1960s.

The name sputnik was inherited unofficially by the larger Spinningdale class and 21 of the type were built by Lewis between 1968 and 1973, followed by the Mark II version or Strathclova class, which had an enlarged working deck and more power and was hailed as having the sea-keeping qualities of earlier trawlers of 120-foot or so in size.

The history of the pocket trawlers is told in 'Sputniks and Spinningdales' by Sam Henderson and Peter Drummond, published in 2011. The authors mention that the 1972-built Spinningdale class trawler *W.R. Deeside* (A.374), under Skipper Bill Wilson, fished out of Aberdeen as a scratcher

The *Spinningdale* of 1968, sailing from Aberdeen on 29th June 1976, was the prototype of John Lewis's successful 86-foot pocket trawler and by early 1982 was reported to be the last scratcher fishing out of Aberdeen. *[J. and M. Clarkson]*

and usually landed twice a week at the port where her catches fetched high prices. She also had the advantage of a power block and net drum which enabled her to trawl over her stern.

The pocket trawlers excelled in the near-water fishery and in the autumn of 1973 some vessels' grossings for short periods at sea averaged more than £1,000 a day, which would have been a good figure for a distant-water trawler. During the same period the Peterhead-built scratchers *Stratherrick* and *Burnbanks* also did well with big shots of codling on the Aberdeen Bank.

Well-known scratchers

The *Burnbanks*, under the command of Bill Mair, was one of the best-known scratchers at Aberdeen during the 1970s and early 1980s. She had been launched as *Midlothian* by Livingstone and Co., Peterhead in 1959 for the Lothian Trawling Co. Ltd. of Granton. However, she was soon renamed *Lothian Leader* after the Registrar of Shipping pointed out that there was already a Thames-based tug named the *Midlothian*. The Livingstone yard's first completion had been the *Strathallan* (237/1956), the first steel trawler to be built north of Aberdeen. The *Lothian Leader* became the *Burnbanks* (A.163) in 1971 when she moved to Aberdeen and where her owners were now registered. The following year the *Burnbanks* rescued the crew of another scratcher, *Vigilance* (A.204), who had abandoned their ship after she caught fire off Peterhead.

The *Vigilance* (149/1958) had been built by Herd and Mackenzie Ltd., Peterhead for the Devotion Fishing Co. Ltd., Aberdeen, and she was something of a rarity in the Aberdeen trawling fleet in having a wooden hull. It was a feature she shared with the 174-ton *Headway* (A.133), built by J. and G. Forbes and Co. Ltd., Fraserburgh and owned by W. Brebner's Nigg Fishing Co. Ltd., Aberdeen. The *Vigilance*'s fire damage was repaired and she passed to D.A.M. Engineers Ltd., Plymouth, later appearing as a trawler on which there had been a 'mutiny' in an episode of the TV drama 'Warship' in 1974. The *Vigilance* ended her days as a derelict hulk at Oulton Broad, Lake Lothing, near Lowestoft, where her remains, along with two former steam drifters and a wherry, could still be seen in 1996.

The *Burnbanks* of 1959 was commanded by Bill Mair and until 1971 had been the Granton trawler *Lothian Leader*. [Aberdeen Journals Ltd.]

Another Peterhead-built scratcher was the *Glenstruan* (A.200) of 1958, which was fitted originally for long-line fishing when she was completed at Alex J. Mitchell's yard at the port's Keith Inch for Peter and J. Johnstone Ltd., Aberdeen. She was the first vessel to be built at the yard and had been designed by Peterhead-born naval architect Stanley Milne. Her maiden trip to fish for halibut off Greenland was filmed by the Esso Petroleum Co. Ltd.'s film unit and the resulting documentary was shown to the public at the time. The *Glenstruan* was later converted to trawling and owned latterly by the Vigilance Fishing Co. Ltd., Aberdeen, whose chairman was Skipper Joseph Wilson. He blamed crewing problems and the prevailing economic situation when his company decided to sell the *Glenstruan* to the Warbler Fishing Co. Ltd., Lowestoft in May 1976.

Offshore oil

By the early 1970s, Aberdeen had become an important supply base for ships serving the rigs prospecting for oil and gas in the North Sea, prompting Skipper Bill Mair to hit out at what he regarded as an intrusion by the offshore energy prospectors on the traditional preserves of the local fishermen. He said the pipeline from the Forties oil field to its landfall at Cruden Bay, Aberdeenshire, was going to cut through one of the inshore skippers' best fishing grounds and he was worried that further pipelines would cause more problems for fishermen.

North Sea oil exploration created a need for offshore standby vessels to lie off rigs in case of emergencies and by early 1974 there were about 100 ex-trawlers, most of them former near-water boats, performing this role although serious concerns were raised that many of these

The *Vigilance* was one of the few wooden-hulled trawlers in the Aberdeen fleet and had been built by Herd and Mackenzie at Peterhead in 1958. [Aberdeen Journals Ltd.]

elderly vessels were unsuitable for such a demanding role in the hazardous North Sea. An Aberdeen scratcher to be converted to a safety ship was George Wood's *Emma Wood*, and had been previously laid-up because of a shortage of crews. She was sold to Putford Enterprises Ltd. of Lowestoft in 1974 and renamed *Northleigh* before starting her new standby role. She had been built in 1957 by Livingstone, Peterhead, and fished out of Granton as the *Teresa Watterston* and *Granton Kestrel* before being acquired by Wood in 1963. The *Northleigh* (A.43) later reverted to trawling and was still fishing in the early 1990s under the ownership of Northleigh Fishing Co. Ltd., Grimsby. George Wood also disposed of the *Boston Sea Hawk* (180/1953) built by Henry Scarr Ltd., Hessle, and in the mid-1980s she spent two summers trawling for herring in the Irish Sea, landing her catches in the Isle of Man while owned by Grant Broad Ltd. At other times of the year she fished out of Fleetwood.

Soaring costs

In contrast to the record catches and excellent quayside prices of 1972-73, there were warnings in May 1974 that the prevailing oil crisis could result in many trawlers at Aberdeen running into debt because of the crippling burden of soaring fuel costs. A prominent trawler manager forecast that the average trawler's annual fuel bill would rocket from £10,000 to £30,000, and this would make many of the older trawlers uneconomic to operate. There had been slumps in the trawling industry in the past but this was the worst yet and trawl owners could see no future signs of recovery.

George Wood laid up its three largest trawlers, the *Braconhill* (274/1956), *Clovella* (238/1957) and *Stratherrick* (237/1960), with the latter departing, under tow, for the breakers at Bo'ness in February 1976 while the other two were sold for demolition later that year. In March 1976, William Wood, managing director of George Wood, brought some cheer to Aberdeen's beleaguered trawling industry as it battled against crippling operating costs when he bought the sister-trawlers, *Carency*, *Gilmar* and *Kinellan*, from the Devanha Fishing Co. Ltd., Aberdeen, which had laid up the vessels six months earlier. Mr Wood said at the time that he was cautiously

The *Gilmar* of 1960 heads out of Aberdeen on 28th June 1976. She was bought, along with her sisters, *Carency* and *Kinellan*, from the Devanha Fishing Co. Ltd. by George Wood in 1976. *[J. and M. Clarkson]*

optimistic about the industry's future, but it was still the worst slump he had known in the sector during his 23 years in trawling.

The *Gilmar* (A.468) of 1960 had been the first of the 104-foot sisters to be completed while the *Carency* (A.573) and *Kinellan* (A.578) followed in 1961. The *Gilmar* had in fact been built at Montrose by John Lewis and the Aberdeen steam collier *Mount Battock* was diverted to Montrose, while northbound from Granton, to tow the *Gilmar* to be fitted out at Lewis's Aberdeen yard, where her sisters were built.

As the Aberdeen trawling fleet declined in number the departure of redundant trawlers under tow for the breakers' yards became a regular occurrence. The arrival of the well-known steam tug *Cervia*, of International Towing Ltd. of Chatham, Kent, to tow the trawlers *Granton*

Falcon and *Strathdon* to Middlesbrough breakers in June 1977 aroused much interest at the port as she had been built at Aberdeen in 1946 as the *Empire Raymond* by Alexander Hall. As the *Cervia* she was a familiar tug on the Thames for many years. Later that year the veteran 243-ton scratcher *Strathisla* (A.391) brought a little cheer when she appeared looking very spruce with a green hull and white line, red boot-topping, white wheelhouse and black-topped red funnel. She had been the Granton-registered *Schiehallion* until 1972 and was built by Livingstone, Peterhead in 1961. From 1974 she was owned by the partnership of Raymond Smith, George Thomson, Gordon Paterson, Alexander Nicol and George Robb, with George Thomson being her regular skipper. However a couple of years later she too fell victim to the depression and was laid up before being scrapped at Bo'ness in early 1980.

The Peterhead-built scratcher *Strathisla* of 1961 returns to Aberdeen after a fishing trip. She was formerly the Granton trawler *Schiehallion*. *[J. and M. Clarkson]*

First-hand

Alfie Freeland had suggested to me that a trip on a scratcher would be an ideal way of gaining a first-hand impression of North Sea trawling, and in April 1979 I made a four-day trip on George Wood's *Craiglynne* (A.324), which had been completed by John Lewis in 1960 for Bon-accord Mutual Ship Stores Ltd. She was managed by Thomas Davidson, whom I had approached about the possibility of making a trip. During the peak year of 1973, the *Craiglynne* was one of the top trawlers in her class and grossed an average of £600 a day during her six to eight days' trips. In that year Aberdeen had a fleet of 120 trawlers but the depression in the industry had taken its toll and by the spring of 1979 this had dwindled to about 55 active vessels.

The *Craiglynne* shot her first trawl 35 miles south east of Aberdeen on Monday afternoon, but despite the fine weather the hauls were disappointing. Gutting and stowing the fish took much less time than normal, allowing the trawlermen to retire to their bunks to catch up with lost sleep as trawling had gone on through the night. Their efforts had been hindered by torn nets and a warp had to be re-spliced after it had snapped during the night. The only other trawler seen was George Wood's *Heather K. Wood* (A.723), skippered by James Bowie.

Most of the *Craiglynne*'s 11-man crew had been trawling all their lives and although they might have been tempted to exchange the hard life at sea for a soft job ashore, they now felt they were too old to make the change and the sea had become like a drug which kept pulling them back. The skipper, Bill Geddes, complained that it was an awful life but felt resigned to trawling because one didn't get two chances in life.

It was a calm sea as the *Craiglynne* approached the North Pier at Aberdeen and I recalled that Alfie Freeland had told me that the nearest he had come to being shipwrecked was when his trawler shipped a heavy sea right aft as she was battling her way across the bar, where seawater meets freshwater, into the harbour in the face of a south easterly gale. He said these south easterlies made Aberdeen difficult to enter and this was exacerbated by the need to go 'slow ahead' when entering port. On that occasion he couldn't make port and had to ride out the gale in the bay.

Above: The John Lewis-built scratcher *Craiglynne* of 1960, on which the author made a fishing trip in April 1979, passes the Round House control room near the entrance to Aberdeen harbour. *[Aberdeen Journals Ltd.]*
Below: The cod-end is swung aboard the *Craiglynne* while fishing off the Aberdeenshire coast in April 1979. *[Author]*

When the *Craiglynne* landed her catch on 13th April 1979 she was one of only 15 trawlers which discharged a total of 127 tons of fish. Fifty years earlier, on 27th March 1929, 1,290 tons were landed, probably the greatest quantity of fish landed in any one day at Aberdeen.

Soon after my *Craiglynne* trip I exchanged notes about life on a trawler with Bill Cottrell, superintendent at the Royal National Mission to Deep Sea Fishermen's mission at the Caithness port of Scrabster. Bill had made a similar trip as a supernumerary on George Wood's *Stratherrick* while based at the RNMDSF's Aberdeen mission. He said it had been quite an education and added that it was surprising to see how well nine to eleven men got on together in spite of the arduous and hazardous nature of the work and the rather basic living conditions on board a trawler.

Aberdeen trawlers were regular visitors to Scrabster, usually for repairs to equipment and to load ice but also for the treatment of crew members' shipboard injuries. I learned from two fishermen of the Lewis-built pocket trawler *Kingsdale* that her skipper preferred to land his catches at Peterhead where seven to eight crew members could do the work of 12 fish market porters at Aberdeen and also increase their share of the catch's profits. Aberdeen was part of the National Dock Labour Scheme, which dictated that only porters could land fish at the market, and their high cost was driving some trawlers, especially those owned on a share basis, to land their catches at the non-registered port of Peterhead.

Crisis

George Wood continued to be optimistic about the future of trawling at Aberdeen in 1979 when it took delivery of the stern-fishing trawler *Louise J* (A.763), which was built by Richards (Shipbuilders) Ltd. at Lowestoft. She contrasted with the company's other vessels which were all side-fishing trawlers, including another acquisition, the *Arctic Crusader* (LH.373), built at Peterhead in 1960 as the *Summervale* for William Liston Ltd., Newhaven, Midlothian. Despite the faith placed in the new boat she was laid up in May 1980 because she was proving unprofitable to operate. This was blamed on low quayside prices, the high cost of fuel and the disastrous impact which cheap, imported fish was having on the Aberdeen industry.

George Wood's *Stratherrick* of 1960 sails from a snowy Aberdeen on 6th January 1970 for her first fishing trip of the year after the port's fleet had been tied up for the Hogmanay and New Year holiday. *[Aberdeen Journals Ltd.]*

By the following February the trawling crisis had deepened. William Wood, managing director of George Wood (Aberdeen) Ltd., announced that the firm's *Carency* and *Kinellan* were being laid up, and he warned that there would be no fishing industry left by Easter if the Government didn't subsidise hard-pressed trawler owners who were grappling with soaring operating costs. He added that imminent talks in Brussels to map out a Common Fisheries Policy were far too late. Sadly, the writing was on the wall for the company which went into receivership in December 1981, along with its associated company, Thomas Davidson (Trawlers) Ltd. The *Kinellan*, which had earlier resumed fishing, was Wood's last operational trawler and was laid up after landing her catch at Aberdeen on 21st December.

After the collapse of George Wood the only scratcher reported fishing out of Aberdeen in early 1982 was the prototype 86-foot pocket trawler *Spinningdale* commanded by Norman Stephen and owned by Williamina W. Forbes and George Craig and Sons Ltd. Craig's company, the North Star Fishing Co. Ltd., and the John Wood Group were now the last remaining members of the Aberdeen Fishing Vessel Owners' Association.

The *Craiglynne* and the *Bracondene* (215/1961) from the former George Wood fleet left Aberdeen under tandem tow in April 1982 for demolition at St. Davids-on-Forth, but others were given a new lease of life. The author was pleasantly surprised to find the *Gilmar* and *Kinellan* going through their survey on the former Everard slipway at Greenhithe on the Thames in January 1984. Later that year the pair were bought by the Milford Haven Fish Merchants Association and were operated from that port by Southard Trawlers Ltd.

The *George R. Wood* was sold to Ghanaian interests in September 1982, while the *Heather K. Wood* (220/1960), built by the Ardrossan Dockyard Ltd., became the *Lady Maria* in 1983, being

The John Lewis-built *Mount Melleray* (216/191) became the *Grampian Fortune* in 1962 and had her career at Aberdeen prolonged after being converted to an offshore standby vessel. She later reverted to fishing and in the early 1990s was line fishing as the *Ayr Queen*. *[Aberdeen City Libraries]*

Trawlers laid up at Palmerston Quay, Aberdeen on 2nd March 1976. The nearest vessel is the 1960-built *Seaward Venture* of Bruce's Stores (Aberdeen) Ltd. which resumed fishing from the port in April 1977 under the ownership of George Craig and Sons Ltd. *[Author]*

operated by Leicester Trawling Ltd., Plymouth. The latter vessel underwent major conversion work resulting in a covered working deck, which radically altered her appearance. She was switched from trawling to long-line fishing and was still active in the early 1990s as the *Dean* of Dean Fishing Enterprises Ltd., London. The *Arctic Crusader* remained at Aberdeen after having been bought by Seaward Fishing Services Ltd. Nearly all the side-fishing trawlers at Aberdeen were now of the pocket type, but an interesting survivor of the more traditional type in the early 1980s was the 162-ton *Bickleigh* (A.201), owned by the Bickleigh Fishing Co. Ltd., Aberdeen. She had been completed by Richards Iron Works Ltd., Lowestoft for local trawl owner Putford Enterprises Ltd. in 1962 and was bought by John McLean of Aberdeen in 1971. However, she is recorded as having ceased fishing from the port in February 1985.

The scratchers had become a memory as Peterhead supplanted Aberdeen as Scotland's premier fishing port and today no white fish is landed at Aberdeen. Auctions had ceased at the fish market by December 2010 because of the infrequency of landings at the port, and the market was later de-registered on 1st January 2013 although the site is still used for the trans-shipment of processed fish.

A view of the Albert Basin at Aberdeen harbour in 1972, looking across from Albert Quay to the Commercial Quay section of the fish market. At Albert Quay is the scratcher *George R. Wood* while the trawlers waiting to land their catches at the market are, from left, *Clova, David John, Mount Melleray, Summervale* and *Emma Wood*. *[Associated Press/Peter Myers collection]*

BOSUN'S LOCKER

58/1

An excellent response to this query: we must be making them too easy as three replies came in one post! Thanks to John Bamforth, Brian Hollman, Christy MacHale, Alan Savory and Tony Smythe.

The wrecked steamer is the *Sussex* (1896/1,117), then owned by les Chemins de Fer de l'État Français. She was built in 1896 by Denny, Dumbarton, for the London, Brighton and South Coast Railway, and used initially between Newhaven and Dieppe, but transferred to Folkestone to Dieppe in 1914, in which year she was put under the French flag. She is seen after she was torpedoed 18 miles west by north of Boulogne by *UB 29* on 24th March 1916 while bound from Folkestone to Dieppe. Of the 53 crew and 325 passengers, at least 50 were lost, some when lifeboats capsized after launching. The dead included the Spanish composer and pianist Enrique Granados and his wife. Not surprisingly, this was the last civilian sailing to Dieppe.

Remarkably, given the loss of her entire bow forward of the bridge, *Sussex* remained afloat and was towed into Boulogne. The photograph may have been taken there, or at Berck at the mouth of the Seine. At least three other views of her in this position are known, two of them showing her beached. The aged, three-masted cargo ship behind her is also aground, and it too may have been damaged.

Sussex was repaired and returned to service under the French flag as a minesweeper. In 1921 she was sold to D. Demetriades, Piraeus and renamed *Agia Sophia*, only to be broken up about a year later following a fire.

As an aside, the book review in 'Record' 58 mentioned Duncan Haws' sometimes unreliable data, and here is a case in point. In 'Merchant Fleets 24' he cites 1st January 1917 for the above incident. This is in fact the date on which the Federal steamer also named *Sussex* was mined. Tony Smythe points out that, used with caution, Duncan Haws' books can prove very useful, and this is something with which the editors fully concur.

58/2

Captain James Anderson tells us that this is the steamer *Ohio* of the White Star Steamship Company, Seattle, USA. On 12th June 1907 while approaching Nome, Norton Sound, Alaska she received ice damage that flooded number 1 hold. A total of 75 people jumped overboard; four died,

the rest were recovered. Nome is shallow and cargo was, and is, routinely landed by barges. In 1909 the ship struck a rock near Swanson Bay, Finlayson Channel, British Columbia and was subsequently beached at Carter Bay where a considerable portion of the wreck was still visible about 15 years ago. The ship was built in 1872 by Cramp of Pennsylvania and was considered the last word in American iron steam ships at that time. The ship was regularly employed between Philadelphia, Queenstown and Liverpool from 1873 until 1895. In 1898 the ship was sold to Alaskan interests. White Star was incorporated in 1905; besides the *Ohio* they had the *Oregon* and *Garonne* plus chartered tonnage. The funnel design is correct for White Star. The ship was 343 feet long and 3,488 gross tons. Notice the after davit of the third lifeboat appears to have buckled.

Wrong *Atlantida*

In the Raul Maya photograph offer in 'Record' 57, photograph number 27 was identified as the Standard Fruit reefer *Atlantida* of 1925. Right name, wrong ship, as the photo depicts the *Atlantida* built in 1921 as *Oriental*. She carried the name *Atlantida* when owned in Montevideo between 1946 and 1951, and was very likely photographed off this Uruguayan port. Interestingly, she was ordered by the United States Shipping Board from a shipyard in Shanghai, Kiangnan Dock and Engineering Works. Under her fifth name, *Kyokko Maru*, she was scrapped in Japan during 1960. Thanks to Ken Bottoms for pointing this out.

59/1 and 59/2

Regular correspondent Alan Savory has asked readers to attempt identification of this semi-submerged ship and its location. The two hospital ships in the middle background date the photographs to the First World War.

SHELL T2s LAID-UP IN LOUGH SWILLY
Captain Michael Pryce

In the aftermath of the Suez Crisis of 1956, tanker owners decided that their smaller tankers had to be replaced by much larger ones, and by 1960 these larger newbuildings were joining their fleets. In 'Fairplay' of 27th October 1960 it was reported that Shell had sold a block of 20 of their older tankers to the British Iron and Steel Corporation (Salvage) Ltd., London, for breaking up. Their sale was announced by Mr. H. Wilkinson, the chairman of Shell Tankers Ltd., at the launch by Vickers-Armstrong of the new 66,790 ton deadweight tanker *Serenia* (42,082/1961) on18th October 1960 at Walker-on-Tyne. Mr. Wilkinson said that the launch of *Serenia* had been

One Shell T2 that did not go to Lough Swilly: following an engine breakdown *Trochiscus* (ex *Fort Matanzas* 1948) was scrapped in the Far East. *[J. and M. Clarkson]*

conducted against the background of a heavy world surplus of tanker tonnage. It would help, he said, if owners took the bold step of scrapping vessels which, because of their size and age, were uneconomical. He then announced that Shell had just decided to scrap, through the mechanics of one single transaction, 20 tankers – none of them over sixteen years old and two several years younger. The company hoped that other owners would emulate their action, and thus quicken the process of dispensing with surplus tonnage.

Three of the tankers were laid up in the River Blackwater, but the majority were laid up in Lough Swilly (see table). They had gathered there from the summer of 1959. It is understood that Shell had sold them for about £70,000 each in October 1960. The other two tankers in the block of 20 sold were *Helicina* (12,167/1946) and *Hyalina* (12,267/1948), both turbo-electric tankers built by Swan, Hunter and Wigham Richardson Ltd. at Wallsend. Both were laid up in the River Blackwater in 1958 and scrapped at Blyth in 1962 and 1961 respectively.

The only T2 not included in the sale was *Trochiscus*, which had broken down on 29th May 1959 and had been towed by Shell's *Halia* (12,183/1958) to Trincomalee on 1st June. She left Trincomalee in tow of the tug *Thames* on 20th June 1959 and arrived in Singapore Roads on 30th and was laid up. She arrived at Hong Kong on 22nd December 1960 for demolition by Chiap Hua Manufacturing Co. (1947) Ltd., Hong Kong, having been sold for £87,000.

The Shell T2 tankers were not the only bulk purchase by BISCO during the year, as they also bought ten Liberties from the United States Government's reserve fleets, seven tankers from BP, and four other tankers from Shell. The four from Shell had been purchased earlier in 1960 whilst idle in the River Blackwater. One of these, *Limatula* (6,476/1950), was

understood to have been the most modern tanker to be disposed of for demolition. Bearing in mind that out of her ten-year life she had been laid up for over a year, it was a sad commentary on the state of the tanker market that such a young ship should be consigned to the breakers. The others were the Dutch-flag *Etrema* (6,162/1936), *Dorcasia* (8,083/1938) and the former depot ship *Nuttallia* (8,341/1945). During 1960 BISCO purchased 243 ships totalling 1,018,801 gross tons, comprised of 70 tankers totalling 649,238 gross tons, 73 dry cargo, passenger and other vessels of 261,516 gross tons, 78 trawlers of 17,957 gross tons and 22 naval vessels and auxiliaries with a total displacement of 90,090 tons. Biggest was the 44,500-ton battleship HMS *Vanguard*, which was allocated to Shipbreaking Industries Ltd. at Faslane. The size of the BISCO 'fleet' awaiting allocation to shipyards could be judged from the fact that by the end of 1960 none of the 20 Shell tankers had yet been allocated, and four of the BP tankers were lying in South Wales waiting for space in the shipbreaking yards.

Tectus sailed from Rotterdam on 23rd March 1960 and arrived at Lough Swilly on the 26th. *Tomocyclus* sailed from Rotterdam on 13th April 1960 and arrived at Lough

Tectus at Cape Town. She was built in 1945 as *Crow Wing*, and was acquired by Anglo-Saxon Petroleum Co. Ltd. in 1947. *[J. and M. Clarkson collection]*

Above: *Tribulus* (formerly *Stones River*) has the assistance of three tugs in May 1959. She is in the Bristol Channel, with South Wales tugs in attendance and may have been going to Cardiff for tank-cleaning prior to delivery for scrapping. *[J. and M. Clarkson]*

Right: *Tomocyclus*, ex-*Capitol Reef*, at Cape Town in April 1953. *[Ships in Focus]*

Bottom: *Trigonosemus* had been built as *Tuolumne Meadows*, named after an alpine flower meadow in the Yosemite National Park, California. *[Ships in Focus]*

Swilly on the 16th. *Tribulus* sailed from London on 11th May and arrived at Lough Swilly on the 14th. *Thelidomus* sailed from Punta Cardon on 19th May 1960 for Old Kilpatrick, and after discharge and tank cleaning, sailed to Lough Swilly to lay up.

The old tankers were anchored off Rathmullen, where in earlier years Admiral Jellicoe had anchored the Grand Fleet after Scapa Flow became unsafe because of German submarines. Rathmullen is at the sheltered entrance of the River Swilly, about halfway down Lough Swilly on the western side. The Irish Coast Pilot Book describes Lough Swilly, 'entered between Fanad Head and Dunaff Head, about three-and-a-half miles eastward, is a spacious inlet extending to its tidal head near the town of Letterkenny, about 22 miles south south westward. It affords secure anchorage for a fleet of the largest vessels. Rathmullen roadstead affords a sheltered anchorage, for with heavy north westerly gales the water here is quite smooth. The depth of the anchorage is about 10 fathoms (18 metres).'

The Shell T2s were generally used to carry crude oil so, after discharge of their last cargo, the ships were thoroughly tank-cleaned, lines washed, and the ships heavily ballasted prior to sailing for lay-up, with the quantity of bunker fuel on board minimised. Because initially their future was uncertain, many had their hulls quickly given a coat of black paint. On arrival at Lough Swilly the tankers were anchored in their designated positions, using both port and starboard anchors, before the ship's machinery was completely shut down and the crew departed. Until sold to BISCO in October 1960, the ships were still the responsibility of Shell, who would have needed to ensure that adequate watchmen and security were provided. After sale to BISCO that responsibility would have transferred, leaving them in charge of whatever local watch keeping

arrangements BISCO cared to make. Even prior to sale by Shell to BISCO, it was clearly the intention that the ships would never sail again commercially, so there was no need to install any de-humidification equipment. After sale to BISCO, they were just awaiting a vacant space in a demolition yard. Local comments that the laid-up tankers were 'much-plundered' would indicate perhaps that local boatmen had no reservations about starting the demolition process early! At the time, the sight of the laid-up tankers in ballast used to draw quite a crowd of viewers, not only from Rathmullen but more particularly from Fahan on the eastern side. Things did not always go perfectly, however, and on 27th January 1961 'Lloyd's List' noted that *Trigonosemus* had broken her moorings in a very heavy gale at 11 a.m. that day and drifted aground on a sandbank, with soft bottom, west of Inch Island at the southern end of Lough Swilly. The Glasgow tugs *Cruiser* and *Campaigner* arrived in Lough Swilly on 1st February and refloated her that evening at 5.45 pm, but she re-grounded west of Rathmullen Pier and was finally refloated by the same tugs at 7.30 am on the 2nd, when they towed her out to sea, bound for the Clyde. However, at 3.55 pm that afternoon, she was reported to have broken adrift from her tugs four miles north north east of Inistrahull Island, showing just a red stern light, drifting with nobody on board, but with the tugs standing by. All shipping was warned by radio. A Royal Navy helicopter was used to put four men aboard her from the tug *Warrior* on the morning of the 3rd and by 11.25 am she was connected up and again in tow of *Cruiser* and *Warrior,* with *Campaigner* in attendance. They arrived in the Clyde at Tail of the Bank safely and she was secured to a buoy by 5.20 pm on the 4th. She arrived at Port Glasgow on 2nd March for demolition.

Although laid-up in full Shell colours, ownership passed to BISCO after October 1960 and Shell held no further interest in

Top: *Tagelus* at Cape Town in September 1952. Her original name was *Ackia*. [Ships in Focus]
Upper middle: *Thalamus*, built as *Fort Raleigh*. [Fotoflite incorporating Skyfotos]
Lower middle: *Thallepus* at anchor. She had been built in 1944 as *Chaco Canyon*. [Roy Fenton collection]
Bottom: *Theliconus*, leaving Cape Town and riding very light. [Ships in Focus]

Above: *Thaumastus*, August 1958.
[Ships in Focus]

Left: *San Leonardo* in Eagle Oil colours.   She had been built as *Bryce Canyon*, and had been sold to Anglo-Saxon Petroleum Co. Ltd. in 1947 as *Turbinellus*, being acquired by Eagle Oil and renamed two years later. In July 1959 the entire Eagle fleet passed to Shell, who repainted but did not rename them. *[Ships in Focus]*

Bottom: Eagle Oil's *San Leopoldo* at Cape Town in June 1955. Built as *Laurel Hill*, she too went through Anglo-Saxon ownership as *Tresus* from 1947 to 1949. *[Ships in Focus]*

the tankers thereafter. With both anchors down, the anchor cables frequently became entwined (or 'foul') as the ships sometimes swung the same way at each turn of tide or wind change. When it came for the time to move them, two tugs were required. One made fast with a towing line at the bows. The other moored alongside just aft of the forecastle and connected an air compressor to the windlass so that compressed-air could be used to weigh first one anchor, then the other, usually after sorting out the tangled cables. The laid-up tankers were dead ship with no steam, so the usual method of raising the anchors could not be used.

Lay-up and demolition of Shell's British-flag T2 fleet					
Name	**gt/built**	**Arrived**	**Laid-up**	**Broken up/arrival**	**Shipbreaker**
San Leonardo (ex-*Turbinellus*)	10,641/44 Portland	6.3.1960	Lough Swilly	Dalmuir 2.9.1961	W.H. Arnott Young and Co. Ltd.
San Leopoldo (ex-*Tresus*)	10,669/44 Portland	6.3.1960	Blackwater	Inverkeithing 6.1.1961	T.W. Ward Ltd.
Tagelus	10,678/45 Mobile	16.7.1959	Lough Swilly	Rosyth 29.6.1961	Shipbreaking Industries Ltd
Tectarius	10,706/44 Mobile	5.7.1959	Lough Swilly	Faslane 28.6.1961	Shipbreaking Industries Ltd.
Tectus	10,689/45 Mobile	26.3.1960	Lough Swilly	Blyth 7.7.1961	Hughes Bolckow Ltd.
Tenagodus	10,661/44 Mobile	18.5.1959	Blackwater	Inverkeithing 3.9.1962	T.W. Ward Ltd.
Thalamus	10,701/45 Portland	18.2.1960	Blackwater	Blyth 5.5.1961	Hughes Bolckow Ltd
Thallepus	10,693/44 Portland	11.8.1959	Lough Swilly	Port Glasgow 2.9.1961	Smith and Houston Ltd.
Thaumastus	10,686/45 Portland	13.7.1959	Lough Swilly	Blyth 3.7.1961	Hughes Bolckow Ltd.
Theliconus	10,691/44 Mobile	8.11.1959	Lough Swilly	Dalmuir 29.5.1962	W.H. Arnott Young and Co. Ltd.
Thelidomus	10,673/44 Portland	13.6.1960	Lough Swilly	Faslane 18.1.1961	Shipbreaking Industries Ltd.
Theobaldius	10,702/45 Portland	31.7.1959	Lough Swilly	Faslane 15.3.1962	Shipbreaking Industries Ltd.
Theodoxus	10,696/45 Portland	11.8.1959	Lough Swilly	Faslane 8.6.1962	Shipbreaking Industries Ltd
Tomocyclus	10,706/44 Portland	16.4.1960	Lough Swilly	Dalmuir 26.5.1961/ Old Kilpatrick 8.1961	W.H. Arnott Young and Co. Ltd.
Tomogerus	10,689/44 Portland	16.4.1960	Lough Swilly	Faslane 9.1961	Shipbreaking Industries Ltd.
Tribulus	10,699/45 Portland	14.5.1960	Lough Swilly	Faslane 9.5.1961	Shipbreaking Industries Ltd
Trigonosemus	10,693/44 Portland	24.7.1960	Lough Swilly	Port Glasgow 2.3.1961	Smith and Houston Ltd.
Trochiscus	10,685/44 Portland	30.6.1959	Singapore Roads	Hong Kong 22.12.1960	Chiap Hua Manufacturing Co. (1947) Ltd.
Trochurus	10,692/45 Portland	16.8.1959	Lough Swilly	Port Glasgow 3.1962	Smith and Houston Ltd.

A fine view of a laden and travel-stained *Theodoxus* putting into Cape Town. Prior to her acquisition by Anglo-Saxon Petroleum Co. Ltd. she had been the *Modoc Point* of United States War Shipping Administration, registered at Portland, Oregon where she was built in 1945. The owner's title changed to Shell Petroleum Co. Ltd. in 1955 and to Shell Tankers Ltd. in 1960. *[Ships in Focus]*

The other Shell T2s

The Shell Group owned five other T2s, *Junon* (10,707/1944, built Portland) and *Minerve* (10,702/1944, built Portland) under the French flag, and *Paloma Hills* (10,632/1945, built Sausalito) *Rincon Hills* (10,635/1945, built Sausalito) and *Pinnacles* (10,641/1944, built Portland) under the Canadian flag. *Junon* was used for floating oil storage at Port de Bouc from 9th March 1961 and arrived at Castellon, Spain in September 1964 for demolition. *Minerve* was used for floating oil storage at Port de Bouc from 8th December 1960 and arrived at Castellon on 2nd April 1964 for demolition. *Paloma Hills* arrived at Hirao in August 1961 for demolition. *Rincon Hills* arrived at Osaka in April 1961 for demolition. *Pinnacles* was sold and converted into the chemical carrier *Alchemist* in 1961, and eventually arrived on 18th November 1982 at Aviles, Spain for demolition.

Top: *Junon* at Cape Town. Built at Portland as *The Dalles*, she passed to Société Maritime Shell via the French Government in 1948. Lasting longer than British-flag T2s, *Junon* was scrapped by Desguaces Maritimos S.A. in 1964. *[Author's collection]*

Middle: The French-flagged *Minerve* began life at Portland as *Donner Lake*, acquired by Shell again through the French Government in 1948. She too ended her days at Castellon. *[J. and M. Clarkson collection]*

Bottom: All three T2s owned by Shell's Canadian tanker owning subsidiary, Deepsea Tankers Ltd., retained their building names. This practice was not uncommon, and British Tanker Co. Ltd. was a notable proponent. *Rincon Hills* was completed as part of a sequence from Marinship which were named after ranges of hills. *[Author's collection]*

A significant number of T2s were extensively rebuilt, either 'jumboised' or converted to bulk carriers or for specialist uses. However, the Portland-built Pinnacles was unique amongst the Shell examples in having a further career, in her case as the chemical tanker Alchemist, seen passing Hoek van Holland on 23rd March 1975. Rheinstahl Nordeseewerke G.m.b.H. at Emden built new fore and midships sections in 1961, retaining her engines which drove Alchemist for another 21 years, longer than her 18 years as a crude carrier. [Malcolm Cranfield]

The T2 builders

No less than 481 turbo-electric tankers of the T2-SE-A1 type were built between 1942 and 1945, and it is remarkable that only four shipyards contributed to this total, of which three were represented in the Shell fleet. These were the Alabama Drydock and Shipbuilding Company of Mobile, Alabama; the Kaiser Company's Swan Island Yard at Portland, Oregon, and the yard of Marinship Corporation at Sausalito, California (which also built another 44 A2 and A3 variants of the design. The fourth yard was the Sun Shipbuilding and Drydock Company at Chester, Pennsylvania, which had largely developed the design.

The Shell T2s appear to have been relatively well kept, even being repainted on arriving in Lough Swilly for lay up, which is in contrast to their war weary appearance whilst with the United States War Shipping Administration. By way of contrast with the photograph earlier, this is Palo Duro, soon to become Shell's Theliconus. Gun tubs are still evident. [World Ship Society Ltd.]